How to Be a Great Catechist

Judene Leon Coon

HOW TO BE A
GREAT
CATECHIST

TWENTY-THIRD PUBLICATIONS

185 WILLOW STREET • PO BOX 180 • MYSTIC, CT 06355
TEL: 1-800-321-0411 • FAX: 1-800-572-0788
E-MAIL: ttpubs@aol.com • www.twentythirdpublications.com

Dedication

I would like to dedicate this book to the Sisters, Mission Helpers of the Sacred Heart of Baltimore, Maryland, who were founded in 1890, for the purpose of evangelization and catechesis. They were pioneers in the field of religious education in this country, and I was blessed to spend more than twenty-five years of my life with this gifted community. To these sisters I owe all that I have learned about this privileged catechetical mission—to proclaim the gospel message to all people.

Chapter 19 has been reprinted from the September, 1985 issue of *The Catechist*, and Chapter 20 has been reprinted from the July/August, 1986 issue of *The Catechist*, a publication of Peter Li Education Group.

Twenty-Third Publications
A Division of Bayard
185 Willow Street
P.O. Box 180
Mystic, CT 06355
(860) 536-2611 or (800) 321-0411
www.twentythirdpublications.com
ISBN:1-58595-274-5

Library of Congress Catalog Card Number: 2003104406
Printed in the U.S.A.

Table of Contents

Introduction

In describing the Mission Helpers of the Sacred Heart, a bishop once said he greatly admired these missionary sisters because they worked with "their heads in the clouds and their feet firmly on the ground." They are sisters who always keep the high goals of their mission before them but work to accomplish those goals in practical, down-to-earth ways, adapting their work to each situation in which they find themselves. This is something we should all strive for as catechists. To be a great catechist means to keep our hearts and minds focused on the inspirational goals and objectives of religious education, while at the same time always attempting to learn more practical ways of reaching those goals.

Today, the book and magazine markets seem flooded with practical materials that offer suggestions for how to accomplish just about any task. "How-to" books and articles are probably among the most popular available. They tell us how to run computers, repair cars, decorate homes, cook meals, tape movies, invest money wisely, and so forth. Every technical product sold today includes a book of directions, some clearer than others. Why not, then, a how-to book for catechists, with practical, down-to-earth suggestions on how to accomplish the goals of religious education in ways that appeal to children today?

How can I more effectively communicate with the youngsters in my class? How can I make the best use of my religion class time? How can I integrate Scripture with my lessons in a variety of ways? How do I utilize the chalkboard, videos, pictures, newspaper articles, the computer, to make my lessons more appealing? How can I review material without boring the children? How can I help them make what they are learning their own? How can I maintain the discipline necessary to present my lesson most effectively? In religious education workshops and conventions, catechists have searched consistently for answers to these and similar questions. This book has been written in response to these questions. Hopefully, it will provide you with some practical suggestions that will help you, as a great catechist, to "keep your head in the clouds, and your feet firmly on the ground."

CHAPTER 1

Preparing the Way of the Lord

How to understand your mission as a catechist

What do you feel when you read the Scriptures about John the Baptist? Do you admire his courage, his self-discipline? Do you think of him as a radical whom you could never imitate? Is there anything you believe you might have in common with this unusual man whom Jesus called the "greatest" of the prophets? Of course...as catechists you share his mission. Like John the Baptist, your work as a catechist is to prepare the way of the Lord in the heart of each child you teach.

Preparing the Way of the Lord
When Jesus was asked to say who John the Baptist was, he quoted from the book of Malachi: "Lo, I am sending my messenger to prepare the way before me" (Mal 3:1). Insert your own name in place of the words "my messenger," and you will see that you do share with the Baptist this great privilege of preparing the hearts of little ones to be open to the Lord. Further, in the book of Malachi this messenger of the covenant is compared to a refiner's fire: "For he is like the refiner's fire...He will sit refining and purifying silver" (Mal 3:2, 3). A group of parishioners who were studying this Scripture reading were puzzled by the concept of God's messenger being like refining fire. They wanted to understand its meaning better, so one of the women visited a silversmith and arranged to observe the process of refining silver. She noted how the silversmith

3

held the silver candlestick he was working on over the fire for quite some time, and she asked why this was necessary. He explained that this process removed all the impurities from the candlestick. She asked further, "How do you know when the process is completed and the candlestick is finally purified?" The silversmith smiled and replied, "Oh, that's easy. I know it's purified when I can see my image in it."

Our Mission as Catechists

As a catechist you are a messenger of the Lord, preparing the hearts of those you teach to be open to God's purifying touch so that Christ's image may be formed in them. The formation of Christ in the hearts of our children is the goal of catechesis, but it is important to keep in mind that we do not do the actual forming. God does it through us. Our part is to be the messenger who helps prepare those hearts to receive God's loving touch and purifying fire. But how can you be this kind of messenger?

Sharing Your Own Faith

The best way you have of doing this, of course, is by sharing your own faith life, your own love of God, your gratitude for God's many gifts, your friendship with Jesus, your love of and fidelity to Christ's Church. Share this personal faith as much as possible when you teach each religion lesson. Sometimes your faith will be shown by what you tell the children about your own faith life. At other times your role as messenger will be shown by the way you present the faith to them. Tell your group, for example, how you have come to know and love Jesus. Share with them stories of your own celebration of the sacraments and what they mean in your life. Don't be afraid to talk with your children about the struggles you may have had in living your faith and how you faced those struggles, or the moments of inner joy and comfort that your faith has brought into your life. All of this will help young people see that faith is not something separate from our real lives, something we only teach or learn about, but that faith is an important part of who we are.

Sharing the Faith of Others

It is also important to share with children the stories of others whom you may know or public figures with whom they are familiar. For example, you can talk about the courage and heroism of those countless persons who worked so hard and unselfishly to help the victims of the

September 11 terrorist attacks, persons like Father Judge, the Fire Department chaplain who gave his life for this cause. Help them learn about the ministry of Mother Teresa and her sisters among the poor, and of those parishioners whose ministry expresses their great love for God and their appreciation of the gift of faith. Point out the dedication of the seven astronauts who died in the Columbia space shuttle in February of 2003. They gave their lives to advance the betterment of mankind. The astronauts represented three major religious heritages: Christian, Judaic, and Hindu; they showed how religious differences need not divide us. In spite of such differences we can be united in a common cause to help others. Events like those just mentioned are usually vivid in a child's mind, and can be perfect opportunities for sharing moving examples of the relation between faith and real life. Use examples from your own life and the lives of other persons as living examples of the faith lessons you are teaching.

Children, too, have faith experiences that can be shared. Whether the children are young or older, use some thought-provoking questions to help them express their experiences. For example: Did you ever feel that Jesus was very close to you? Have you ever thought: "What a wonderful world God has created for us"? Have you ever felt comforted by God when you were sad? Have you ever felt especially proud to be a Catholic? If so, is there someone you know who reminds you of Jesus? Young children usually enjoy sharing in this way. Older children may be a little more reticent about it. It is best not to pressure them. Expressing their faith experiences privately in a journal is another way that can help them recall God's action in their lives.

Forming Minds as Well as Hearts

If *formation* is our goal as catechists, how important is it to share *information* with those we teach? How is knowledge of the faith related to appreciation for it and the living of it? Our ministry involves preparing children's minds as well as their hearts, for the two go together. What we love and what we choose to do in our lives is based on what we believe and understand about life. St. Paul understood this when he urged the Philippians: "Let the same mind be in you which was in Christ Jesus" (2:5, NRSV). To help those we teach to know and understand life and the world as Jesus saw and understood it—the awesomeness of God, how we are called to love one another, the great gifts God has given us in Jesus, in the Church—all of this will help form Christ in their minds so that their hearts will be moved to love and live as Jesus did. In the following chapters you will find many how-to suggestions for helping children come to know and understand the mysteries of their faith in an enjoyable way. At the same time remember that, like John the Baptist, you too are a privileged messenger, striving to prepare these children for God's purifying work of forming Christ in them. Through this process God forms Christ more fully in your own heart as well, so that we all, catechists and catechized alike, may come to reflect the purity of God's image within us.

Summary

- Like John the Baptist, your work as a catechist is to prepare the way of the Lord in the heart of each child you teach.
- We prepare those we teach to be open to God's purifying touch, so that Christ's image may be formed in them.
- The formation of Christ in the hearts of young people is the goal of catechesis, but God forms them through us, his messengers.
- We help prepare the hearts of the children we teach by sharing our own faith life and the faith of others, and by allowing the children to share their faith experiences as well.
- As catechists, we are called to prepare children's minds as well as their hearts. What we love and what we choose to do in our lives is based on what we believe and understand about life.

Questions for Reflection

In what way do I experience my mission as a messenger of God to the children I teach?

How do I perceive my goal as a catechist? How can I accomplish this goal?

What is the relationship between formation and information in catechesis?

CHAPTER 2

Communicating the Message

*How your environment, manner, and method of teaching can
improve how you communicate with your religion class*

Communication is probably one of the most talked about and read about concepts in our world today. In an age that has developed so many new, efficient ways to communicate—from telephone, radio, TV and satellite, to electronic mail, faxes, and the world wide web—we might expect more dialogue, more understanding, and more cooperation among people. But effective communication is hard to come by, and modern technology, rather than helping, can sometimes impede or depersonalize it. For catechists especially, improving communication skills is extremely important. *The General Directory for Catechesis* tells us: "The catechist is essentially a mediator. He facilitates communication between the people and the mystery of God" (article 156).

Do you experience yourself as a mediator? A communicator? Here you are, standing before your religion class. You have worked hard to acquire the best possible background in Scripture, liturgy, and theology. You have spent many hours preparing your religion lesson. Yet you may feel frustrated as you stand before the children you teach because you can't seem to get your presentation across to them. You wonder what simple things you might do to better reach their minds and hearts. How can you improve your situation so that it will be more conducive to learning? Let's look at three areas that affect the way you communicate with your children, and see how we might improve them. The areas are: environment, manner, and method.

Your Environment

I know of catechists, myself included, who have taught in every kind of surrounding: in church pews, in choir lofts or sacristies, in rectory basements, on back porches, in a parishioner's restaurant (closed on Sunday morning), in living rooms, on beaches, in hallways, on patios, or in the traditional classroom. The seed of God's word can be planted in any environment. And each has the potential for being made into the "good soil" in which that seed can grow. Much of what I suggest here will apply to the traditional classroom, but think of the circumstances in which you teach, and adapt the ideas as they fit your situation.

The arrangement or set-up of your meeting space may seem like an insignificant matter, yet it can seriously affect the learning process. Arranging your room so that each child can see and hear you to the best advantage is important. If you have children with hearing or visual problems, be sure they are placed in seats that enable them to participate. In a fourth grade class I visited recently, Cecelia, who was both blind and crippled, sat in the front row directly in front of her catechist. Here she felt close to the catechist and could receive the special attention she needed. If you have some children who delight in being the center of attention, you may find it more helpful to place them near the back of the room where they will be less distracting to others, and away from those "friends" with whom they constantly converse.

If you teach in a traditional classroom with desks or chairs that stretch across the room in neat rows, you may want to rearrange the room. The seating I have always found most helpful is a semi-circle, which gives a feeling of closer contact between catechist and children and children with one another. If you choose to use this arrangement, be sure of course, to move each seat back into its proper place before leaving. Tape a number to each desk before moving it so as to speed up the replacement process at the end of your session. I have also seen rooms where rows of desks are alternated, so that no boy or girl sits directly behind another. If the seats are stationary and you have no choice in arrangement, move among the children from time to time. They will be more aware of your presence among them and feel that you are talking *with* rather than *at* them.

Ask yourself this question about the area in which you teach: What do the children feel as they enter this room? Does the room radiate peace, warmth, friendliness? Or do they get a sense of being overwhelmed and distracted by all the "busy work" around the room? I have entered rooms with so much clutter that they made me feel dizzy. Pictures, charts, or seasonal decorations were everywhere, and some had mobiles hanging from the ceiling. Traditional classrooms often have desks overflowing with books, pencils, and papers, or computers and other audiovisual equipment filling the room. While some decoration is needed to give the room a warmer atmosphere and often even reinforce learning, it is important to remember that when there is too much to see, we often see nothing.

If you are in a schoolroom, or some other area occupied by another group, how can you improve the surroundings without overstepping your boundaries? I once taught a seventh grade class in a cluttered room something like the one I've just described. Since it belonged to another teacher, I felt I could do little to change it. However, I rearranged the seats by pulling them into a semi-circle in the center of the room, away from all the clutter, marking each one so that I could return it to its proper place before leaving. I also used an easel to display some appropriate pictures and words that the children could focus on during my presentation, so the surroundings would have less impact on them. If you are fortunate enough to have a room of your own, by all means decorate the room simply. Use some of the available space for posters or charts for prayer, for teaching, or for review, but don't overdo. If you use some type of chalkboard or whiteboard for your sessions, don't fill it up. You will find that these simple arrangements help the children listen with less distraction and focus on the lesson you are presenting to them.

Your Manner
Children today are surrounded by fast action. They can sit and play computer games or watch fast-paced TV shows or movies for hours at a time with rapt attention. Even cartoon shows for the very young are full of drama and action. Remembering this may motivate you to improve your manner of presenting your religion lesson. A dull religion session just doesn't stand a chance. If you want your group to believe that the

Good News is really good, you will need to smile more. If you want them to realize that their faith is alive and exciting, you will need to present it in that way. You can't just memorize material from a book, no matter how good the text is. Your religion lesson needs to be prayed over and reflected on, until you become so full of it that it spills over enthusiastically to those you teach.

Be sure you speak loudly and clearly enough for every child in the room to hear. Ask the children to do the same. Some children speak or respond to questions in such a soft voice that the others miss their message. Insist that each child speak loudly and clearly enough for others to hear, or repeat their response for the rest of the group.

The pace at which you teach is important, too. You need to know your lesson so well that you can pass quickly from one idea to another without a great deal of hesitation. If your pace is too slow or if your presentation is disconnected, you will lose the children's attention. Once their attention is lost, it is difficult to pick it up again.

You also need to be alert. Don't become so wrapped up in the lesson itself that you don't notice the children you are teaching. I recall an economics professor I had in college. He was a brilliant man and had a wonderful background in his field. Yet the students did not enjoy his class. The reason was because he paced back and forth in front of the chalkboard speaking to us, yet hardly ever having any eye contact with us. We felt he was teaching the subject but not us.

Analyze, too, how you handle responses to your teaching. Instead of simply nodding yes or no to the children's remarks, comment on them. Encourage their participation and show that you are truly interested in each contribution. Pupil participation doesn't simply mean letting children speak and act. It means interacting with them. If you require written work to be handed in from time to time, write a few encouraging words on each paper before returning it, to show that you have read it with interest.

Lastly, do you teach the children as a group, or do you try to reach each girl and boy as an individual, on her or his own level? Children will respond with attention to the degree that they sense you care about them as individuals. Try to learn each child's name as quickly as possible, and call each one by name—before, during, and after your session with them. Make large name tags for younger children the very first week you meet with them. Let them decorate these and wear them several times until they learn each other's names. Older children can make their own when they come to your first session. Be sure to have them print their name in large letters so they can be easily read.

Listen carefully to questions or comments made by the children. Certainly there will always be some who will make comments to draw attention or ask questions to "throw you off the subject." But I have found that most often, children are sincere in their comments or generally interested when they ask questions. I recall one fourth grade class in which the boys and girls were learning the commandments. The catechist asked one day, "What is the ninth commandment?" Ann answered, "Thou shalt not covet thy neighbor's husband." The catechist assumed immediately that Ann was looking for attention. But in reality, Ann was sincerely applying the commandment to her situation.

With regard to questions, if you can't immediately see the relationship between a child's question and what you are teaching, don't assume that the child is trying to throw you off track. Try to draw him or her out more. A child's mind is very imaginative and often will see connections that may not be evident to you. Be patient and also take time with those who are slower to grasp an idea you are teaching. Invite other youngsters to help explain the more difficult points.

Your Method

How you go about presenting the Good News to your children will depend on what that message means to you. Are you interested enough to learn it well and make it a part of you? Or do you constantly have to refer to your book? I have seen catechists who held on to their textbook during their entire presentation, and constantly stopped to refer to it. The group you teach needs to know that the lesson comes from within you, not simply from between the pages of a book. You are the faith "lived," and your inner understanding of the faith and your experiences in life can have a great impact on those you teach. Try to present the material without hesitation and with conviction. Let the children see that you are not afraid of questions, even those you can't answer. If you handle them calmly and with assurance, they will feel more comfortable about their own questions. Questioning is a normal process as we grow in faith. Children may be unaware of this and feel guilty about asking. Your matter-of-factness in responding to their questions will put the children at ease. If you are unsure of an answer, simply let them know that you will do your best to find an answer for them. Then remember to follow through on your promise.

Most religion textbooks today have a world of information and help for catechists. Background is provided on the psychology of the child and on the theology of the lesson. Both goals and objectives, outlines and developed plans, suggested activities and audio-visuals are presented. Make use of all this helpful material and by all means don't discount the importance of activity in your lesson. Activities are not meant to be distractions or simply busy work for those you teach. They are meant to help you get your basic message across in a way that involves the group: with Scripture readings, stories, dramatization, pictures, charts, music, games, chalkboard illustrations, art, videos, and tapes. Young people respond to activities according to their personalities and mood. One child may miss an essential point you made when talking to the class, but may pick it up when it is repeated in a story. Another may be captivated by a picture you are showing or the dramatization of a Scripture reading. Still others may learn best from videos or tapes that complement your lesson. So, vary your activities. Use music for one lesson, games for another, and the chalk or white board for others. Don't become too "predictable." Children, like adults, love variety and surprise.

Finally, take time, even it if is only five minutes before the end of the session, to go over the important points of the lesson again. List these on a chalkboard or chart and have the children repeat them one last time. They need not remember every point of the lesson, but they should at least be able to explain in their own words one or two of the essential ideas they have learned.

If all of this seems overwhelming, don't be discouraged. Remember that even for Jesus, the perfect teacher, there were those who simply did not understand him or his message. It was not until the coming of the Holy Spirit that the apostles began to comprehend Jesus and his mission. Because of the Holy Spirit, the divine communicator who is there with you, blessing your efforts, you are not alone as you stand before your group of children. Praying for the help of the Holy Spirit should always be a part of your religion class preparation. It is only because of the Spirit that you can even hope to communicate God's Word to the boys and girls you teach. St. Ignatius once advised: "Pray as if everything depended on God, and work as if everything depended on you." This is a good motto for catechists and a perfect formula for communicating God's Word.

Summary

- Three areas to examine for improving communication are your environment, your manner, and your method.
- Your environment. Arrange the area in which you teach so that it is most conducive to each child's learning—pleasant and comfortable but not cluttered.
- Your manner. Present your religion lesson with enthusiasm, at a good pace, and be alert to the children's attention and responses, encouraging their participation and interacting with them. See children as individuals, calling each by name. Respond positively to their questions.
- Your method. Let the message of "lived" faith come from within you, rather than from the textbook. Handle children's questions with calm assurance. Don't be afraid to admit you don't know the answer to a question. Use the helpful resources found in your textbook. Use a variety of activities to get your message across. Take time at the end of your session to review important points of the lesson.
- Remember the Holy Spirit is there, helping you to communicate God's message.

Questions for Reflection

What can I do to improve the setup of the area where I teach?

Do I interact with the children in my religion class as individuals or as a group?

How can I improve my manner of presenting the religion lesson?

In what way am I an example of "lived" faith to those I teach?

CHAPTER 3

Fitting Into the Whole Picture

*How you can work together with other catechists
to present an integrated parish program*

I love working on jigsaw puzzles. When I do, I follow these three steps. First, I keep the picture on the cover before me constantly as a guide. Second, I assemble the outside frame. Third, I try to study the color and shape of each piece so that I don't force it into a spot where it doesn't belong.

Keeping the Picture Before You

"What is that chart on the wall?" a new catechist once asked me when she noticed the Scope & Sequence poster in her classroom. I explained that it was a Scope & Sequence chart which outlined all the material that would be covered in our religion program for grades one through six, including what she would be covering in the third grade that year. She was delighted with the chart and the "bird's eye view" it gave her of what the children had learned and would be learning. I encouraged her to become familiar with the Scope & Sequence because it is something like keeping your eye on the cover of a jigsaw puzzle box as you are attempting to put the puzzle together. If you are unfamiliar with the Scope & Sequence, you never really see the whole picture of what your parish religion program is trying to accomplish or where you fit into that picture. The Scope & Sequence will help you see what the children have already learned so that you know what to build on. It will show you where they are going so that you can be sure to cover what is necessary for them to move on to that point. It will also help you see where the truths of our faith connect with one another so that you get a sense of wholeness, which is important to convey to those you teach.

Catechists can easily become so focused on their own group of children that they lose the sense of being part of a larger whole. While the textbook is only meant to be a tool and should be adapted to your group, ignoring the text or getting too sidetracked can make it difficult for the catechist who will be teaching your group the following year. If pieces of the puzzle are missing, the picture is never complete.

Some religion series include a total Scope & Sequence chart as well as a yearly one within each individual catechist guide or on a separate chart. If you have not seen the Scope & Sequence for your religion series, ask your coordinator or DRE to get one for each of the catechists. If your religion series does not publish one, perhaps your catechists could meet together and outline for themselves what is being taught each year so that you get a total view of the program. Keep this picture of the whole before you constantly as you are teaching. Each catechist will have a broader sense of the faith, a deeper insight into the connections between what we believe and what we live, and a greater experience of working together.

Building on the Frame

After studying the cover of a puzzle box, what is the next step you take? I have always found it helpful to begin by building the frame of the picture. This is the easiest part because each piece has at least one flat side that identifies it as an outside piece. Once the frame is built, it is much easier to add on the other pieces. The individual Scope & Sequence for your grade is like the frame for your year's lessons. It will outline the main topics you will be covering and the sequence to follow in presenting them, although it will usually allow flexibility in fitting liturgical lessons into the Church year. Most Scope & Sequence charts will show you how Scripture, doctrine, prayer, and liturgy are integrated into the lesson. Familiarize yourself with your own Scope and Sequence chart. It will help you see how these "pieces" of the religion lesson build on one another.

Joining the Wrong Pieces

Do you ever find yourself trying to fit more into your presentation than is called for in the text? While it is important to share your own personal faith experience with the children, as catechists we need to be careful not to impose on them ideas and feelings that don't fit their age level or circumstances. If you have studied the Scope & Sequence for the entire religion program, you will notice that there is a gradual enrichment in each of the important topics as the children move from one grade to another. This progression in the truths of the faith is not something that publishers put into their texts randomly. Much consultation goes into deciding what the children are ready for at each grade level. Trust their guidance in this matter. If you have a section in your textbook on the psychology of the child, compare this with what is being covered that year on a particular topic. The two should correspond.

For example, while the names of Father, Son, and Holy Spirit are introduced in the lower grades, the children's way of grasping ideas is still too concrete to understand the concept of "Blessed Trinity."

There may be references to the Church in a second grade lesson, but this is not the time to teach the "four marks" of the Church. While Scripture is incorporated into every lesson in most texts, it is not until the sixth grade that most of them begin to discuss literary forms. Learn as much as you can about the "color and shape" of your children's minds and hearts. It will help you to know which "pieces" of the faith they are ready to receive. Trying to cover every point of a doctrine before the children are ready is like attempting to force a puzzle piece into a spot where it doesn't belong.

Looking More Than Once

Take time then, at the beginning of the year, to look over the Scope & Sequence with your DRE and the other catechists. You may find it helpful to share among you the points of the faith that each of you is strongest on. Then take time around the middle of the year to review it once again. Do you still have a view of the "whole picture"? Have you covered the essential points that new ideas can be "attached" to? Have you avoided forcing into your lesson any ideas that the children may not yet be ready for? If the answers to these questions are all positive, you can be fairly sure you've found where you and the children you teach fit into the whole picture, and you've put together much more than just a pretty jigsaw puzzle.

Summary

- The Scope & Sequence of your religion series will help you see what your group has already learned so that you know what to build on. It will show you where they have been and where they are going so you can be sure to cover what is necessary for them to move on to the next point.

- The Scope & Sequence will show you how truths of the faith are connected and give you a sense of the wholeness of the religion program. Following your individual Scope & Sequence builds the "frame" for your year's lessons.

- Try to discover as much as you can about the "color and shape" of your children's minds and hearts so that you will know which "pieces" of the faith they are ready to receive. Imposing ideas and feelings that don't fit the children's age level or circumstances is like trying to force a puzzle piece into a spot where it doesn't belong.

- Examine the Scope & Sequence at the beginning of the year, and review it again around the middle of the year to see if you are covering the necessary material.

Questions for Reflection

How familiar am I with the Scope & Sequence for our religion program?

How does it help to experience my place within the whole parish religion program?

What basic points of Scripture, doctrine, prayer, and liturgy do I need to cover this year?

In which areas should I be careful not to give the children more than they are ready for?

CHAPTER 4

Using Your Time Wisely

How to make the best use of time and still cover the essentials

Probably no one values time more than a catechist. As you prepare for your weekly religion classes, you are repeatedly faced with the question: "How can I cover this material adequately?" The goals of faith formation have come a long way from teaching catechism questions and answers, and your teacher's manual has grown proportionately thicker as it has improved in trying to help you accomplish those goals. It offers you numerous choices, and you hate to sacrifice any one of them because each seems so important in presenting the whole Christian message. Your manual reminds you that pupil participation, though time-consuming, is essential to real learning. What's the answer, then? Should you rush through your lesson in order to cover it all? Should you spend more time on pupil participation? How can you use your meeting time to the best advantage?

Plan Your Religion Session Well
Probably the most important time saver is a well-prepared presentation—one that moves quickly from one point to another without seeming to rush. Go over your religion lesson in advance to make certain you are truly familiar with it. Choose as many concrete examples as possible to get ideas across. Textbook writers try to present situations that appeal to the average group, but you may find that some of the examples are not as appropriate for the children you are teaching. Choose

those that resemble your youngsters' environment and are suited to their age. Children raised in a country environment will respond to different images than suburban children or those from a large metropolitan city. Abstract images that appeal to you as an adult may be confusing to children. For example, as an adult the concept of the Mass as a sacrifice offered to God can have great meaning. A young child can better understand the Mass as an exchange of gifts between God and us. This image provides them with a concrete mental picture and takes less time for them to grasp. As they grow older they will be able to absorb more abstract descriptions.

Another example is that of the Church. The five images of the Church proposed by Avery Dulles in his book, *Models of the Church* (Doubleday & Company, Garden City, NY, 1974)—institution, mystical communion, sacrament, herald, and servant—are insightful and thought-provoking concepts for adults but are too difficult for younger children to grasp. However, presenting the Church as a family of believers is an image with which they can identify. Most manuals today suggest concrete examples such as these to convey abstract truths. However, you still need to think them through carefully in light of the particular children you are teaching. Try to see and understand these ideas as they would, and make the concept even more concrete by illustrating it with audiovisual aids when possible.

Organize Activities in Advance
Your kitchen table may look like mass confusion as you prepare for your weekly lesson, but do get those outlines, pictures, flash cards, charts, or other aids organized before you step into your religion session. We all have good intentions about preparing at least a week in advance and doing it at a leisurely, thoughtful pace, but that dream does not always become reality. At times, you may have only fifteen or twenty minutes for your final preparation. If this is the case, use some of that time getting things in order and try to reflect on your lesson as you do this. In one parish in South Carolina faith formation sessions were held between Masses. Many catechists came in early to set up their rooms and then celebrated Mass after their religion session ended. This worked out well for them since most of the children also attended the later Mass. If you teach between Masses, and if children have time to remain

after your sessions, you may prefer to celebrate an earlier Mass so you can be free to talk with the children afterwards. Whatever the circumstances or time for your group to meet, take at least fifteen or twenty minutes to get your mind and your materials organized in advance so that the lesson can be presented smoothly.

Wherever you teach, it is helpful to place visual aids—pictures, flashcards, newspaper articles, and so on—face down on a desk or a table nearby where they will be easy to reach. Put them in the order in which you'll be using them and print lightly on the back of each one what the word or picture is so that you won't have to fumble looking for the right one. Before your religion session begins, if you are using a chalkboard, make sure it is clean and that chalk and an eraser are available. If some children in your group come early, ask them to be responsible for having the materials in place.

If you plan on using games or other activities, have all your materials ready at hand. Needless to say, all audio-visual equipment should be checked out and plugged in ahead of time. Set any videos, CD's, and so on, at the place where you wish them to begin. Chairs should be arranged ahead of time so that every child will be able to see well. Taking care of all these incidentals in advance saves valuable time and also helps you to maintain discipline.

Take Attendance Quickly

Your religion program may require that you take attendance each week. If your group is small, this is not time consuming. You might even do it mentally and fill in your attendance sheet after the session. With a larger group, however, rather than calling roll yourself, have a helper do it while you are getting your things in order beforehand. Or use the name tags you have made for the children. Place these in a box near the door and have the children put them on as they enter. If the name tags are not adhesive, let them attach a small piece of masking tape to the back. The masking tape can be discarded and replaced each week if necessary. Name tags like these take less time to put on and remove than those with pins. Tags left in the box belong to the absentees. But be sure to check at the end of your meeting to see if everyone has picked theirs up. With older children try having two slot-charts at the door, or two boxes, one empty and the other with name cards. As they enter, the youngsters remove their name from one chart or box and put them in the other to show they are present. A final option is simply to pass the attendance sheet around and have the children check their own names.

Post Key Words and Assignments
When new words are being introduced in the lesson, instead of having children take time to copy them down as you present them, have them written ahead of time in a corner of the chalkboard or on a chart. As the children enter the room, have them look at these key words and either copy them down, or find them in their books before you begin your session. Then simply refer to them at the appropriate time. The same may be done with an assignment. Have it written on the chalkboard or chart so that the children can copy it before you begin teaching. This will help them be alert for any information they may need to complete the assignment. Be sure to remind them about the assignment before they leave.

Give Clear Directions
One of the secrets of good communication is being able to put yourself in the place of those to whom you are speaking. Don't take for granted that because something is crystal clear to you, it will also be clear to your listeners. This is especially important when you are giving directions. Even adults can have difficulty in this area. Nothing is more frustrating than buying something that says "assembly required" and then finding that the directions are unclear. Many of the "For Dummies" books written today are not really for "dummies." They are simply books that have made a real effort to give simple, clear directions for doing things. Poor directions often result in wasted time. So if you want to save valuable teaching time, give clear, adequate directions. For example, if you want a child to take a specific seat in the front row, don't say simply, "Sit up here in front." Point to or place your hand on the seat you would like the child to take and say, "Please take this seat."

If you are working with very young children, put yourself in their place. Listen to your directions with their ears and see what you are describing with their eyes. For example, if you are working on a project to make a booklet and you give each child an 8.5" by 11" sheet of paper and instruct them to fold it in half, what will happen? Some will fold it lengthwise and some will fold it horizontally in half. Even adults might respond in this way. It is better with children, if at all possible, to show them what you mean. One second grade catechist was instructing her class about making a prayer booklet. This can be confusing because pages are not numbered in the correct order until they have been assembled. Instead of telling them to cut out the pages, color them, and staple them into a booklet, she explained and demonstrated it one step at a time. She first instructed them to cut the pages on the dotted line and then showed them how to do it. Then she folded the booklet she was working on so they could see exactly how it was done. After the children had folded their own booklets, she had them go through it with her to make sure they had the pages in the correct numerical order. Then, the books were ready to be stapled together with the help of the assistant catechist.

Be sure, also, when working with very young children, to avoid giving multiple directions at the same time. For example: "Mary Ann, go to the chalkboard, point to Jesus in the picture, and tell the class what Jesus is doing." This may sound simple to you, but it is three separate directions for a young child. Try saying it this way. "Mary Ann, please come to the chalkboard." When Mary Ann is there, say, "Can you find Jesus in the picture?" Then when Mary Ann has pointed to Jesus, ask, "What is Jesus doing there?"

With older boys and girls who are doing work in their text or activity book, encourage them to read the directions carefully before they begin working. You may want to go over the directions with them and ask if they have any questions.

Ask Clear Questions

Be sure that you are clear in asking questions as well as giving directions. In one class, a catechist asked: "If someone were to talk badly about Jesus, would you defend him?" I noticed the hesitation the children had in answering. Then finally, a light struck David, who was seated in the back, and he said "Yes." At first the question had puzzled the children. They weren't sure if the catechist was asking if they would defend Jesus or the person who talked badly about him. David finally realized she meant Jesus.

Avoid Excessive Responses to Questions

A great deal of time in your religion sessions can be taken up responding to questions the children ask. I am in no way suggesting that their questions should not be answered. But be careful that you don't elaborate excessively in your responses. We all have "favorite" truths we enjoy discussing, and we can be tempted to spend too much time on some minor unrelated point simply because it is one of the topics we enjoy most talking about.

On the other hand, don't try to hurry through the lesson in a rushed manner in order to cover everything. This can give the impression that what you are teaching is not important. Rather, emphasize the most important truths to be covered. Most textbooks today have summary sections which highlight those truths. If there are a few additional facts you feel were not covered, but should be, you might take five minutes at the end of your presentation to challenge the children to help you find them. Have them quickly look over the lesson in their textbooks to see if there is any truth mentioned there which you didn't explain in class. This helps them to review briefly what they have learned. Then have them read together the omitted section, and take a few minutes to answer any questions they might have concerning it.

Once you have a personal knowledge of your children and how they respond to you, you will find what works best for them. Use this knowledge to adapt your presentations to the group. From time to time, review how your religion sessions are going, to see if there might be better ways to plan or organize your sessions so that no time is lost on nonessentials. In doing this, your material will be more than adequately covered, and you will find it much more satisfying and enjoyable for yourself, as a catechist.

Summary
- Planning your religion lesson well is the most important time saver. Become familiar with it and choose concrete and familiar examples to get ideas across.
- Have your materials organized, marked, and ready to use.
- Take attendance quickly, whether using name tags, charts, or simply calling roll.

- List new words to be introduced, and assignments on a chalkboard or chart ahead of time.
- Give clear directions. Try to visualize and listen to your own directions. Avoid giving multiple directions to younger children.
- Ask clear questions and avoid elaborating excessively about "favorite" but unrelated topics in your responses to children's questions.
- Avoid hurrying through the lesson, as this can give the impression that what you are teaching is not important.

Questions for Reflection

Do I take time to plan my religion lesson really well?

How can I better organize my materials so as not to waste time when presenting my lesson?

Can I improve my method for taking attendance?

In what ways can I improve the way I give directions and ask or respond to questions?

CHAPTER 5

Putting It All Together

*How to make your religion lesson a part of you
and a part of the lives of those you teach*

One thing we learn very early as catechists is that if we want our teaching to be effective, it is not enough to quickly read over a lesson once or twice before presenting it. The gospel message will never become a part of the lives of our children if it has not first become a part of our lives. Scripture suggests the importance of this in the book of Ezekiel. Before sending Ezekiel to bring God's word to the house of Israel, the prophet is given the command to "eat the scroll" placed before him. "Son of man, eat what is before you; eat this scroll, then go, speak to the house of Israel" (Ez 3:1). This command meant that Ezekiel should make God's word a part of himself before attempting to present that word to God's people. Ezekiel's response was: "I ate it, and it was as sweet as honey in my mouth" (Ez 3:3). How can we "eat" and "digest" the lesson we are going to teach so that it is no longer something separate from us, but rather becomes a very part of us? And can we make it "sweet as honey" not only for ourselves, but for those we teach as well?

The Need for Prayer

First and foremost, of course, in order to accomplish this we must begin with prayer. In one of the Church's traditional prayers to the Holy Spirit, we pray that God "instruct the hearts of the faithful by the light of the Holy Spirit." If we truly believe this, what better way can we begin to prepare our lesson than by praying for inspiration—asking the Spirit to "instruct us" and help us make this lesson part of ourselves, so that it becomes "as sweet" as God's word became for Ezekiel?

Focus on the Central Message

Once we have asked God's help, we're ready for some other steps. Several days before your class begins, read over your lesson to discern what central theme, concept, or attitude is being presented. This may be easier to find in some lessons than in others. For example, the Church may be presented as a body, a family, or a community. Another session may focus on the Mass as a family meal, a sharing of gifts, or a community celebration. A lesson on Jesus may stress his importance as the light of the world, as friend or brother, as savior, or as a teacher. Or another may center on a theme like caring for creation, healing, forgiveness, God's promises, prophecy, vocation, or our life journey.

Whatever the central theme is, once you have discerned it, reflect on it for several days. Try to see and hear things in light of this theme. For example, if your lesson is about forgiveness, be alert to notice any newspaper or magazine articles about forgiveness that you might share with the children. Keep your eyes open for pictures from magazines, newspapers, brochures, calendars, or the computer that might be used as analogies or to build a story about forgiveness. Songs you might hear on the radio, incidents of forgiveness portrayed on TV, especially programs you know would be of interest to the children, possible stories about forgiveness that you have received in your e-mail—all of these can be helpful.

Above all, look for opportunities to share your own faith experiences, or those of family members or friends, about forgiveness. Take note of situations among children who are the same age as those you are teaching. Notice how they relate to one another, how they forgive or don't forgive. You may not use all the information you garner for this particular lesson, but it will help you to "think" and "feel" forgiveness—to catch the spirit of what you want to convey to your youngsters.

Prepare a Theme Notebook.

A project you might find helpful in preparing for lessons is a theme notebook. An ordinary notebook binder with pocketed dividers can be used. Title each pocket with one of the themes you will be covering, for example: creation, life, freedom, person, friend, light, prayer, family, responsibility, community, courage, etc. Or if you wish, just prepare one pocket for each of the lessons you will be teaching. Place in each pocket any pictures, articles, words of songs, stories, that you think might be useful in teaching that topic. You may also want to use a concordance to research Scripture quotes on your theme so that you can have them on hand. List these on a sheet of paper and insert them in the pocket along with the other items. You will find that having all these resources collected in advance can be a great help in preparing your lessons, especially on those days when you have less time.

An example: for a lesson in which Jesus is presented as Friend, these are some of the things I collected in a theme notebook:

• a newspaper article with a picture of a group of girls: an American and two other girls from central America. All of them had been prisoners of guerrilla fighters in a Central American country. When the American girl was finally offered her freedom, she refused to leave unless her two friends were released with her. At first, the guerrilla fighters refused, but they finally gave in and all three girls were released;

• a magazine article entitled "A Friend of the Poor" about a layman from East St. Louis, Illinois, who earned this title by his tireless dedication to those who die alone with no living or caring relative, and by his volunteer work as a member of the St. Vincent de Paul Society;

• another newspaper page entitled "True Friends" in which several persons, including a 12-year-old boy, describe what they consider characteristics of a true friend;

• a greeting card for a special friend, or a note you have received from a friend;

• the names of two books about true friendship that most children would be familiar with, for example, *The Giving Tree* by Shel Silverstein, and *Charlotte's Web* by E.B. White;

• the lyrics of two contemporary songs: "You've Got a Friend" by James Taylor and "That's What Friends Are For" by Dionne Warwick;

• the following list of scripture references about friendship: Job 6:14; Proverbs 17:17 and 18:24; Sirach 6:7 and 37:1; and John 15:15.

Practically speaking, not all themes will be as easy to find material for, but anything you can gather in advance for a particular topic will be of great help.

Outlining Your Lesson

Once you have a sense of or feeling for the theme you are presenting, you will then be ready to read over your lesson again, noting where you can bring it to life by including some of the material you have gathered. Outline the important points you want to cover in each part of your lesson. Your manual will help you do this by suggesting certain steps to follow in your presentation. Some series use a three-step plan, others expand the lesson to five steps, but each one will cover three basic processes: an orientation or introduction to the topic to be covered, a presentation of the new material, and an assimilation process that will help children to integrate and express the material they have learned.

Introducing Your Religion Lesson

Almost all texts use some incident from the child's own life to introduce the lesson. This may take the form of questions, a story, a game, a picture study, etc. But it is always intended to call forth something from within the child's own experience, something to which the new material can be related. This part of the lesson is necessarily brief. Once the minds and hearts of the children are pointed in the right direction, move on to the next step.

Presenting Your Religion Lesson

In the next step, begin immediately to relate what you have just discussed with the children to the new material you will be teaching. The presentation of the lesson should weave together several elements: Scripture, doctrine, liturgy, and witness.

If you are using a Scripture story, be sure to read it over prayerfully beforehand. Using your Bible, look up what events precede and follow the incident so that you understand the background of the story and can better present it in context. If the story is recounted a little differently in other parts of Scripture, read each account and note the similarities and differences.

Use flash cards or write key words on the chalkboard or on a chart to help children focus on and remember important points of doctrine or liturgy covered in the lesson. As far as possible, try to weave the doctrinal points you are teaching throughout the Scripture story as you relate it. Draw out examples from the children of how to live what they are learning. Make the examples as specific as you can. "I will love my neighbor this week" or even "I will be kind" is not concrete enough. "I will try to make friends with someone in my class who seems lonely" or "I will try to be quiet when Mom has a headache," or "I will not join in when others make fun of Joey," are specific examples. Above all, include experiences from your own life as one of the elements of your presentation. Children are always eager to hear stories about you, what you think, and what you feel. Share with them your own personal love of Jesus, what your faith means to you, and how you live it out. You are a much more important "textbook" than the one you hold in your hands. Incorporate teaching on the liturgy wherever it fits into your presentation. For example, when you tell the story of the ten lepers and emphasize thanksgiving, remind the students that the word for our Sunday liturgy celebration is Eucharist, which means thanksgiving. We, the Church community, are like the leper who returned to give thanks. We gather together every Sunday to worship God and to express our gratitude for God's many gifts to us.

Assimilating the Religion Lesson

It is not uncommon for catechists to run out of time before finishing their presentation, usually just at the point when the children seem ready to begin assimilating the material. Yet we know that assimilating the material, and learning to express it is the real "finishing point" of the educational process. While it is true that children today seem to be more adept at expressing themselves, they still need help with this in their religion sessions. Allow at least five minutes at the end of your session to have the youngsters summarize and review briefly what you have taught. Encourage them to express it in their own words, so that they will be able to share what they have learned with others. Let them use flash cards, pictures, the chalkboard, puzzles, games, dramatizations, or whatever is helpful in outlining the main points of the lesson. In Chapter 17, you will find suggestions for using these materials in this way. Your manual will also offer suggestions for this, and most will provide a number of optional activities so you can choose the ones best suited to your group.

Whatever method you use, always keep in mind that you are a "living textbook." The enthusiasm and love of God which you bring to the children as you prepare your lesson will reinforce for them what you have presented in spoken or written word. The General Directory for Catechesis reminds you of this: "No methodology, no matter how well tested, can dispense with the person of the catechist in every phase of the catechetical process. The charisma given by the Spirit, a solid spirituality, and transparent witness of life, constitutes the soul of every method" (article 156). If you have truly made your own the gospel message you are teaching, if you live it as fully as you can, and have done your best to prepare and present the religion lesson, it will surely become a part of their lives as well.

Summary
- The gospel message we present will never become a part of our children's lives if it has not first become a part of ours. Ask the Holy Spirit to make this gospel message a part of your life.
- Reflect on the central theme of your religion lesson, and see and hear things in the light of it. Be alert to find pictures, articles, songs, stories, and so on, that will help you present this theme. A theme notebook can help organize the material you collect.
- Outline the points you want to cover in each part of your lesson.
- The introduction uses experiences from the child's life.
- The presentation of the lesson weaves together Scripture, doctrine, liturgy, and witness.
- Assimilating and expressing what they have learned is the important "finishing touch" of your religion lesson.
- Keep in mind that you are a "living textbook," and more important than any method of teaching.

Questions for Reflection
What do I do to help the gospel message become a part of my life?

Do I remember to pray to the Holy Spirit for guidance?

Where can I look for ideas to help me communicate the theme of the religion session?

How can I improve my presentation?

In what ways am I a "living textbook"?

CHAPTER 6

Being Creative with Scripture

How to use a variety of creative ways
to effectively present Scripture in your religion lessons

Think back to a time in your life when you received a letter from someone you loved very much. The letter may have been from a friend, a parent, a spouse, or a relative. Did you treasure that letter? Why? Words contain something of the person who speaks or writes them. Their words make them present to us in some way, especially if those words come from the heart. When we speak of Scripture as the word of God, we are saying that it makes God present to us. This is why the Church treasures it so highly and why the Council Fathers at Vatican II said: "The Church has always venerated the divine Scriptures just as she venerates the body of the Lord, since from the table of both the Word of God and of the Body of Christ she unceasingly receives and offers to the faithful, the bread of life" (Document on Revelation, art. 21). Scripture, then, should certainly be an integral part of your religion lesson. Virtually every religion textbook today incorporates Scripture into its material, but how can you present it creatively and in a variety of ways?

If there is anything our modern culture teaches us, it is that there are many ways of doing the same thing. Having children read the Bible story from their textbook is only one of the ways Scripture can be presented. There are others you can use to lend interest and variety to your religion sessions.

Storytelling

Storytelling is probably the oldest form known to us of passing on important truths. We never seem to tire of this form of learning. As a child I wondered why so many adults attended our children's Mass on Sundays. I found out later that it was because they, too, loved to listen to the many fascinating stories our pastor, an author of children's story books, told us during his sermons. So, instead of having your children read the Scripture stories from their texts, why not ask them to lay aside their books while you tell the story to them in your own words? As you prepare your lesson, remind yourself that the biblical characters mentioned in the stories had many of the same human feelings and needs as you and those you teach have today. Begin by placing your story in a particular setting. Does it happen in Jerusalem? in Galilee? in the temple? in the fields? Use maps, drawings, or pictures to convey this sense of place to the children. Tell the Scripture story as if you were there yourself. What do you see? What do you hear? What do you feel? What might the persons in the story be seeing, hearing, or feeling? If there are crowds mentioned in the story, talk with the children about who might have been in the crowd. What might these persons have been thinking or feeling as they saw Jesus and heard his words? Help the children to realize that these biblical characters were real persons like themselves. In telling the story don't be afraid to use gestures and different voice tones to make it more expressive. Use pictures, objects, charts, or the chalkboard to illustrate what is happening. For example, if you were telling the parable of the mustard seed (Matthew 13:31,32) you might bring in some actual seeds, easily obtained in a plant shop. Show the children how tiny they are. If you cannot obtain the seeds, draw a tiny seed on the chalkboard and then a large tree with little birds in it, to illustrate its growth as Jesus depicted it in the parable. The sketch need not be an artistic creation. All you need is something simple to help the children focus on the story.

Dramatizations

Children also love to dramatize. Some stories lend themselves easily to spontaneous dramatization. You might read the story while the children act it out. A favorite for this is the story of the Good Samaritan (Luke 10:29–37). Another is the story of the finding of Jesus in the

Temple (Luke 2:41–52). One time, when a third grade class in southern Maryland was acting out this story, the little girl who took the part of Mary really put herself into it. When she came to the part where Jesus is found in the Temple, she put her hands on her hips and in a rather scolding voice asked: "Where yo'all been, boy?"

Other stories may need some advance preparation. You might prepare by asking some volunteers to read a story to be dramatized in a future lesson. Take time to go over the story with them, giving them as much background as possible to help them understand the setting of the story. If the characters' names are not given in the Bible, have a suggested list ready, and let the children select a pretend name for each character. Talk with them about what the lesson is that the story should convey so that their manner and their presentation will get this across to the audience. Then help them decide how to best dramatize the story. If they wish to make props or costumes to wear, be sure to keep these simple. Have all of this in readiness when your session begins so that the dramatization goes smoothly. After the dramatization, take time to discuss with the group what they learned from it.

Scriptural Art

Another way to present the story is to have the children read it over quietly to themselves, noting the message that the story is conveying. Then invite them to draw a picture of what they have read, and call on volunteers to use their drawings to teach this lesson to the others in the group. If the story has several scenes to it, let the children work in teams, each doing a scene and then presenting the pictures in sequence as they tell the story. For example, if the story is the multiplication of the loaves and fishes, each child might draw one of the following scenes: Jesus telling the apostles to feed the crowd; the young boy presenting his loaves and fishes to Jesus; the people seated in groups of fifty and eating; the apostles gathering up the remains of the food into baskets and laying them at Jesus' feet. If you have a very small class, you might invite each of the children to explain her or his drawing.

Puppet-Talk

Young children in particular respond well to puppets. Use some simple hand puppets as narrators to tell the story that is being presented. If the story includes only one or two biblical characters, use the puppets to portray these characters themselves. Most Christian bookstores or even general department stores sell puppets that can be used. Puppets of characters from books, TV, or computer games that the children are familiar with, are easy to find and can be very effective to use in telling a story. Or, if you prefer, make some simple puppets yourself out of brown paper lunch bags, socks, or felt material. If time permits, you might even have the children make some of their own and encourage them to use the puppets to share the story with their families or friends.

Storywriting

Many youngsters like to write stories. You may want to read or tell the story dramatically in your own words, and then invite them to act as biblical writers, putting the story into their own words as if they were telling it to someone for the first time. Call on volunteers to share their stories and point out how each one has put something of himself or herself into the narration, just as the biblical writers did.

Creating a Newspaper

Printing a newspaper section about a Scripture story can be fun as well as an effective learning tool. Following a lesson on the Christmas story from Scripture, a seventh grade group worked on composing a newspaper issue of the event. They entitled the paper, "The Daily Miracle." The youngsters divided into groups and each worked on a special section of the paper. They did drawings of the nativity scene, the wise men on their trip to Bethlehem, and a map of the area where Jesus was born. Others wrote articles: "Savior Is Born in Stable," and "What We Know About Mary and Joseph." "The Story of the Wise Men" included an interview with the three visitors to Jesus. Still others composed letters to the editor: "Babies Wrapped in Cloth" and "Well Water Rationed Because of Scarce Rain." Another wrote an editorial about what the future of this child might hold. Some wrote a recipe for "Baby Jesus Chocolate Cookies," and another an advice column, responding to a question of the innkeeper who sent Mary and Joseph to the stable. One of the girls even contributed a fashion article on camel skin coats, oak staffs, and ladies sheepskin blankets! During the week the written material was all put together and typed up on a computer and copies were made of the drawings. Then the newspaper was assembled and each youngster received a copy to take home to their families. One copy was enlarged and put on the bulletin board to share with other groups. The girls and boys were delighted with their success. As well as enjoying the project, they gained insight into the very real world of biblical times. Similar papers might be done about events like the Last Supper, the Resurrection, or one of Jesus' miracles.

Creating a Puzzle

After presenting a biblical story, or having the youngsters read it quietly to themselves, ask them to make a list of some of the important names and words that relate to the message of the story. For example, a puzzle on the story of the finding of Jesus in the Temple might list words like Jesus, Mary, Joseph, temple, teachers, third, listening, surprised, searching, returned, wisdom, grace, obedient, Nazareth, and so on. Write these words on the chalkboard and work with the group as a whole to place these words in a crossword grid form and number them. For example, the word listening might be a word across and you might build the word temple down from the "t" and the word Nazareth from the "n," and so forth. Divide the youngsters into groups and have each group create a crossword puzzle clue or question for one of the words. Write these clues on the chalkboard in the correct order. Then erase the words in the puzzle and see if they can answer them from the clues alone. Let those who guess an answer come up and write it in the space where it belongs.

Another method would be to use the puzzle activity as an assignment to reinforce what the youngsters have learned in class. Give each one a list of the important words covered in the story, and have them work out a puzzle at home. Ask them to do one blank puzzle and one with the answers. The following week, have them exchange their puzzles and see if each one can complete a puzzle. Then share these with the rest of the group.

Scripture Videos

There are numerous scriptural videos available for use in religion programs today. If you choose to show one of these, give the children some background on the story before showing it. Then give them certain things to be looking for as they watch the video; this will help them stay more focused. For example, if you are showing a video of Jesus' agony in the garden, you might ask them to notice which three apostles stayed closest to Jesus in the garden, or who came to arrest Jesus, or what Jesus said to Judas when he approached him in the garden. After showing the video, lead the group in a discussion. Some videos provide questions for this. If they do not, prepare some of your own ahead of time. Encourage the youngsters to share what they have seen in the video with their family and friends.

Reading the Story

There is nothing wrong, of course, with having the children read the story from their texts, as long as this is not the only way Scripture is presented. Young children, especially those who have just learned to read, seem to enjoy this. Point out any illustrations that accompany the story and discuss these with the children as you go along. With children in the middle grades, you can vary the method of reading the story by assigning speaking parts to individuals and letting the whole class read the narrated part together as a chorus. With the very young who still cannot read, you may, from time to time, choose to simply read the story to them with great feeling.

There are many other ways of presenting Scripture to youngsters. Have them portray characters in the story and do a dramatic reading as we do in our Holy Saturday liturgy, or find examples in the newspaper of modern day versions of Scripture stories. Tell part of a story and have them provide the ending. Have them do a word collage of the story, using the same names and words as you would in the crossword puzzle. Let them write a poem or a song about the Scripture passage.

However you choose to present Scripture to your group, be sure that it is done with simplicity and reverence, and with as much variation as your time and circumstances will allow. Give the Bible itself a place of prominence in your classroom, and encourage the children to create a Bible corner of their own at home.

Summary

- Scripture, the Word of God, makes God present to us. Use Scripture in a variety of ways, such as: storytelling, dramatization, scriptural art, puppet-talk, storywriting, creating a newspaper, and creating a puzzle.
- Read the Scripture stories to the children with great feeling, or have them read it, noting and discussing the illustrations as they go along. Assign speaking parts and let the whole group read the stories together.
- There are many other ways of presenting Scripture; however you choose to do it, always present it simply and reverently.

Questions for Reflection

How conscious am I of God's presence in the words of Scripture?

Do I take time to read and prayerfully reflect on the scripture passages that are part of my religion lesson?

How can I more effectively present Scripture to the children I teach?

CHAPTER 7

Joining with the Parish Family

How to involve those you teach
in the liturgical life of the Church

Can you remember back to your childhood when one of the most important things you needed was to feel a part of the group? The first day you were dropped off at school? The ages around 10 through 12 when you formed a "club" with your playmates? Those adolescent years when being accepted by the group determined what you wore, how you spoke, and where you went? In today's mobile and insecure world, it is probably more important than ever for the children you teach to experience a sense of belonging—not only to their natural family, their group of friends, but to their church family as well. How can you help make that a reality? One way is by introducing those you teach to the liturgy, and motivating them to become involved in those liturgical moments when we gather as a community, to express our worship and share our faith with the whole parish family. Familiarizing them, too, with the rituals that have been passed on in our Catholic "family" over the centuries will give them a greater sense of belonging.

Presenting the Mass

Most religion series include lessons on the Mass in each grade, and sometimes a whole year's work is devoted to various aspects of the liturgy. In presenting the Mass to children, it is important to stress the following: the Mass is a Catholic family celebration; its purpose is to join together with the faith community in praising and thanking God for the many gifts we have received and in bringing to God our shared or personal needs. It is an open expression of our faith in a loving God, in one another, and in the world. Remind the children that Christians consider Sunday the first day of the week, not the last. It is the day on which we receive God's grace and strength to live out our faith during the coming week.

Catholic Rituals

Children also need to become familiar with the rituals that are a part of our Catholic liturgical life. Try to integrate these into your lessons whenever possible. For example, when you teach Scripture or simply read Scripture together, use the signing of the cross on the forehead, lips, and heart that the priest uses before reading the gospel at Mass. Point out to the children how through this signing, we ask God to be in our minds, on our lips, and in our hearts, that we too, may proclaim God's words to others. Encourage the children to participate in this signing whenever they are at Mass, or whenever they read the Bible alone or with the family.

Introducing or Reinforcing the Sunday Readings

If your sessions are held on Sundays between Masses, invite the children to listen carefully to the Sunday readings. Ask those who have already been to Mass to explain briefly what struck them in any of the readings. If possible, let your opening prayer flow from the readings. If the children attend Mass after your religion session, you may want to go over one of the readings with them and explain briefly or discuss with the children what it might mean for them. Using a child's lectionary would be helpful, especially with younger children.

You might wish occasionally to plan for the children to do a simple dramatization of one of the gospel readings either at the beginning or end of your religion session. Stories like: Jesus calls Peter and Andrew (Mt 4:12–23) from the Third Sunday in Ordinary Time; Jesus cures a leper (Mk 1:40–45) from the Sixth Sunday in Ordinary Time; or the visit of Nicodemus (Jn 3:14–21) from the Third Sunday in Lent (all from Cycle B) are examples of stories that can be easily presented and then followed by a short discussion.

The Offertory Procession

Remind the children that the gifts we contribute to the Church each Sunday symbolize the gift of ourselves. To help them express this meaning invite them, as an opening prayer for one of your sessions, to bring a small gift that symbolizes them in some way (a stone, a small crust of bread, a pencil, a flower, etc.). Have a simple procession around the room and conclude the procession in front of the crucifix where the children can lay down their gifts with a simple prayer such as "I give myself to you, Jesus." Be sure to bring a gift of your own and join the children in this ritual.

Water, Wine, and Oil

In sessions on baptism, the children learn about the symbolism of water. Why not take them to visit the baptismal font to have them experience blessing themselves with the holy water? Acquaint them also with the priest's action of blessing and mingling the water and wine to be consecrated during Mass. Discuss with them the significance of the beautiful words the priest prays at this time: "By the mystery of this water and wine may we come to share in the divinity of Christ who humbled himself to share in our humanity." What a profound prayer this is! We are asking God to share with us more deeply God's life (represented by the wine) which we received in baptism, as Jesus shared with us our human life (represented by the water).

In lessons on reconciliation, you may wish to recall the peace gesture at Mass where we express our reconciliation with those around us. In lessons on baptism, confirmation, or holy orders, bring in a small container of oil, and anoint each child's forehead so they may experience this rite. Explain the different types of oil used in the sacraments and the blessing and healing that the oil signifies.

The Great Amen

Write the word Amen on the chalkboard or on a chart and point out to the children that it means "Yes" or "I agree." Ask them to notice the Great Amen the next time they go to Mass, when as a whole community we sing or pray this prayer with all our hearts. Explain to them that we are accepting all that the priest has done at Mass: accepting the bread and wine which symbolize us, changing it into Jesus, and offering this

Gift to God our Father as an expression of our love. Remind them that by responding "Amen" when they receive the Eucharist, they are saying, "Yes, we believe this is the Body and Blood of Jesus."

The Sign of Peace

Ask the children if they understand what the priest means when he invites us to share a sign of peace before communion. Discuss with them the importance of receiving Jesus with a heart that is at peace with everyone. Recall for them Jesus' words: "If you bring your gift to the altar and there recall that your brother has anything against you, leave your gift at the altar, go first to be reconciled with your brother, and then come and offer your gift" (Mt 5:23,24). Have the children offer a sign of peace to one another as your closing prayer.

Rites of Christian Initiation

If your parish has a well developed Rite of Christian Initiation, talk with the children about some of the rites that it includes. The Rite of Acceptance, for example, where the participants are invited and accompanied from the entrance of the church into the midst of the community, is a powerful sign of the great privilege it is to be a member of the Catholic community. You may wish to act out this ritual with the class and then ask them to share how they might feel if they were a catechumen or candidate experiencing this rite.

Signing with the Cross

Another powerful ritual you may want to dramatize is the signing of the five senses suggested as an additional rite of acceptance. In this rite, the sponsors sign each catechumen or candidate with the sign of the cross on the ears, eyes, lips, heart, shoulders, hands, and feet, accompanying each signing with a short prayer such as:

"Receive the sign of the cross on your ears so that you may hear the voice of the Lord."

Invite some youngsters from an upper grade to act as sponsors to give the blessings, or act as the sponsor yourself. Have the children think of one loving way they might use each of these senses after having them blessed.

Of course, the most impressive of all the rituals is the baptism of the catechumens at the Easter Vigil. Have a sharing session, if possible, and invite a child or an adult who has been newly baptized to come and tell your class about their experience. Let your group make cards of welcome and encourage them to make the newly baptized person feel a real part of the parish family. Invite the newly baptized to pray together with you and the children. If possible, invite them to share refreshments with you afterwards.

Experiencing and understanding these rituals of their parish family will give those you teach a greater sense of "at homeness" in the faith community, and hopefully will lay the foundation for a fuller participation in their adult years in the liturgical life of the Church.

Summary

- Involving children as much as possible in the parish's liturgical life will give them a greater sense of belonging to the parish family, and will prepare them for fuller participation in their adult years in the liturgical life of the Church.

- Stress the Mass as a Catholic family celebration in which we join with the faith community in praising and thanking God, and in bringing God our shared and personal needs. Integrate Catholic rituals into your lesson whenever possible, for example, the signing of the cross and accompanying prayers, on forehead, lips, and heart, that the priest uses before reading the gospel; the priest's prayer at the mingling of the water and wine at Mass; the anointing with oil; and the sign of peace before communion.

- The Great Amen is our way of saying "Yes" or "I accept" to all that the priest and the assembly have done at Mass. In receiving the Eucharist we show that we believe that this is the Body and Blood of Jesus we are receiving.

- Discuss Sunday Mass readings and integrate them into your prayers when possible or prepare some simple dramatization of them, followed by discussion. Remind the children that the gifts of money offered at Mass are symbols of themselves. Demonstrate this with a short procession and presentation of gifts at the beginning or end of your religion session.

- Familiarize the children with some of the rites of Christian initiation used in your parish, e.g. the Rite of Acceptance, with its welcoming and blessing aspects. Invite a newly baptized child or adult to talk to your group about their baptism experience.

Questions for Reflection

How does the liturgy help me to experience a greater sense of belonging?

In what ways can I better participate in the liturgy?

What more can I do to help the children I teach to love and participate in the liturgical life of the parish?

CHAPTER 8

Worth a Thousand Words

How to find and creatively use pictures in your religion lesson

As catechists, we probably have heard the old Chinese adage, "One picture is worth a thousand words," so often that we have grown tired of it. But do we really take those words to heart? From time to time, we do make use of videos in our lessons, but what about other types of pictures? Some time ago, I was doing research on St. Augustine for an adult group I was teaching. Suddenly, a picture popped into my mind. It was one I had seen over forty years ago in a high school text. St. Augustine was pictured poring over a Bible with one hand on his heart and an ecstatic expression on his face. For some reason, the picture had captured my imagination, and it helped me recall the story of Augustine's life, especially the passage from Romans (13:13–14) which had been the turning point in the saint's life. That picture had spoken very many, if not a thousand, words to me.

Making Use of Text Visuals

Why is it that all major religious education texts today are full of vibrant pictures and photographs to accompany their lessons? Those who prepare the texts are aware that pictures reinforce and give deeper insight into what we read about. Pictures are not there simply to adorn the catechist guide or the child's text. They are meant to be teaching tools, just as the printed words are, and aids to help the children remember what they have learned.

Starting Points for Stories and Discussion

Textbook visuals can be used in a number of ways to enhance your teaching. Whether you are using contemporary pictures or religious scenes from the text, take time to examine these with your group. Young children often enjoy giving names to the persons in a contemporary illustration. Ask children, whether young or older, to place themselves in the contemporary or religious scene so that they might get a sense of what is being portrayed. Let them take turns answering questions about the story, suggesting what the persons might be thinking or feeling, or why they might be doing what the scene suggests.

Once I observed a class studying the story of Jesus lost in the Temple. The text had an excellent drawing of the moment when Mary and Joseph appeared to find Jesus. It showed Jesus reverently touching the scrolls of the Law, the amazement of the Jewish teachers, and the joy on the faces of Mary and Joseph as they saw Jesus. So much could have been learned by simply studying the picture carefully for a few minutes, yet the catechist never referred to it at all. Nor was any reference made to another picture in the introduction of the lesson, showing little children running joyfully to Jesus, and Jesus' arms extended in welcome. It was a beautiful, reassuring picture of Jesus' special love for children.

Pictures showing how the faith can be practiced are especially helpful as discussion starters. Ask "behind the scene" questions to bring out the circumstances of the situation portrayed. For example, in a third grade session on "Our Church as a Community," a text showed a drawing of a parish group, parents and children together, gathering and packing food, clothing, and other items for victims of a fire. You might talk with the children about how the family may have seen the story of the fire on TV, or read about it in their church bulletin. Perhaps they got together after Mass one Sunday and decided that they should do something as a family to help. But what if some of the children had something else planned with their friends for that day? Ask "Do you think it was hard to make the choice they did to help? Why or why not? Do you think their action was worth the effort and sacrifice they made? Why? What do you think Jesus would have done?"

Other Picture Aids

But don't limit your use of pictures to those in the textbook. Many parishes provide catechists with illustrated biblical scenes and maps, pictures and charts of the Mass, the sacraments, prayer, saints, Scripture, and so on. How often do you use these? They can be invaluable aids in presenting your lesson, in holding the children's attention as you are teaching, and in helping them remember the essentials of the religion lesson.

Start a Picture File of Your Own

In addition to these religious pictures, it is helpful to start a collection of your own pictures to use with your lessons. These are easily obtainable from magazines, newspapers, brochures, calendars, and even from some of the "junk mail" you receive each day. Computers also provide many clip art pictures that can be used in teaching. Make a simple file of your own with the pictures, categorizing them in whatever way is most helpful to you. For example, nature, people, Bible, Jesus, saints, community, Church, sacraments, commandments, prayer, and so forth. Or file them according to which lesson you will use them for. Here are some pointers you may wish to keep in mind as you select and use pictures.

- If your pictures are not large enough, take the time to pass them among the children and give each child ample time to study them.
- Be sure the pictures are cut evenly and mounted neatly on construction paper.
- When selecting pictures, look at them through the eyes of the children you will be teaching. A group of teenagers talking together may appeal to junior high youngsters; kindergarten children may be more drawn to a picture of young children playing together.
- For younger children, choose pictures with as little detail as possible, so that they can focus on the point you wish to make and not be distracted by non-essentials.
- If you post pictures on the wall or board, put them at the children's eye-level, not yours.
- Study pictures reflectively before using them. Let your imagination flow and think of all the points you might make about them. Try to anticipate any questions the children might ask and be ready to answer them.
- In choosing religious pictures, look for those that are reverent yet realistic. Avoid those that are overly sentimental or give religion a "fairy tale" quality.

Techniques for Using Pictures

Once you have selected pictures for your group, use a variety of ways to present them. Following is a list of suggested uses. Choose the ones that you would feel most comfortable with.

Picture Study. A large picture is best for this activity. Post the picture in the front of the room where everyone can see it clearly. Ask the children to study it quietly for a few minutes. Then ask questions that will help them understand what is happening in the picture. For example, in a lesson about the Eucharist, you might use a picture of the Last Supper and ask: Who do you see in the picture? Does Jesus look sad or happy? Why do you think he looks this way? What words did Jesus say over the bread? Over the cup of wine? Put yourself in the picture. Where would you like to be seated? Why? When do you see these actions of Jesus repeated today?

The Name Game. After completing a unit in which you have used multiple pictures, this activity can be useful as a review at the end. Post the pictures on the chalkboard ledge and ask the children to think of several appropriate titles for each one. List these titles above each picture and then have the boys and girls select the one they think is best for each picture, telling why they chose it. A picture of the birth of Jesus, for example, might be entitled: The Light Has Come, God's Gift to Us, The Birth of a King, A Savior for the World. Older children might also contribute titles of their own. A picture of a baptism might be entitled: Becoming a Child of God, New Life, or Entering God's Family.

Picture Story. Choose a picture with people in it. Build a story around it that shows how the people practice what the children have learned. With older youngsters, have them complete the story you have started. For example, if your lesson is about honesty, choose a picture of two boys talking. Begin telling the story and ask the children to decide on an ending for it. Begin the story in this way: "Jerry, a young boy about your age, is talking with his friend Mike. Jerry is telling Mike that, more than anything right now, he would like to have a copy of the videotape *Mario Brothers* because all of his other friends have one. After school that day, Mike and Jerry decide to stop in at Walmart on the way home. Looking around in the tape department, they notice there is no salesperson around. Jerry sees a copy of the tape and says to Mike...." Stop the story there and let one youngster continue. Then, at other critical points in the story, give other children a chance to continue it, until the story is finished. Finally, lead them in a discussion of their parts of the story.

Picture Sequence. In some religion lessons, where a series of pictures has been used to demonstrate a sequence of events, you can use the pictures to review the lesson. For example, in a lesson on the passion of Jesus, you might show pictures of the Last Supper, Jesus' arrest, Jesus before Pilate, the carrying of the cross, and the crucifixion. Afterwards, line up the pictures along the ledge of the chalkboard, but do not put them in order. Call on a child to come and choose the first event, explain it to the group, and place it at the beginning of the line. The next child chooses the second, and so forth until the pictures are all in the proper order and the story is completed.

Picture Collage. This technique works well especially with younger children. Choose some small pictures that portray the special response you wish from a lesson, for example, kindness to one another, reverent prayer, or an attitude of forgiveness. Also choose some pictures that clearly illustrate the opposite response. Make sure the message of each picture is clear. Paste these on posterboard or newsprint to make a collage. After teaching your lesson have the children examine the collage and take turns coming up and drawing a circle around a picture that demonstrates the response you are looking for. Have them cross out those that illustrate the opposite response, explaining the reasons for their choices.

Picture Challenge. Teaching values and clear thinking is important, especially with older children. Pictures of magazine ads can help you do this. Cut out some of these ads and paste them on construction paper. Car, jewelry, and clothing ads are often good for this. You may wish to arouse curiosity about them by drawing question marks around them. Show an ad to the students and ask if they have seen it. Most of these ads have some kind of slogan or punch line that suggests an underlying value or attitude, for example a Wendy's ad showing items from their 99¢ menu that suggests: "It's the best 99¢ you can spend" or the ad for Basic cigarettes which says: "The best things in life are Basic."

Invite individuals to either challenge or support the ad, explaining their reasons for doing so. You may wish to have them take sides, one group in favor and one against. Lively discussions can result.

Picture Report. In a lesson where you have used the story of an event in Jesus' life, post a picture of this event where all in the group can see it clearly. Ask them to study it carefully, recalling the details of the story. Then suggest that they write a newspaper account describing the incident. Or, if you prefer, explain the difference between a news report which states facts and an editorial which expresses an opinion, and have them choose to write one or the other.

Picture Meditation. Some pictures can be used effectively as aids to prayer, for example, pictures of the Good Shepherd, of Christ's passion, of Mary or the saints, even of nature scenes. With older children you might sometimes use pictures of homeless children or families living in poverty for a meditation on helping others, and so on. When using a picture for this purpose, be sure that it conveys a sense of reverence. Post this picture where it can be seen by all. Stand quietly in the back of the room and ask the children to look at the picture as you lead them slowly in a prayer. Ask them to enter into the prayer with you as much as possible, perhaps imagining themselves as part of the picture. Play some quiet music in the background as you very slowly and reverently reflect on the picture, pausing between each thought. Invite the children to contribute their thoughts after you have completed yours.

Picture Quiz. As a summary of a textbook unit, instead of giving a traditional "test," challenge your group with a picture quiz. Select one picture from each lesson you have taught. Post these on the chalkboard or on a chart and write a number over each one. Give each boy or girl large sheets of paper and ask them to draw a small square for each picture you have displayed and put its number in the center of the square. Then around each square, ask them to write short comments explaining important points they remember about the lesson. For example, around a picture of Christ's agony in the garden, they might write: "Jesus suffered like us and for us. We too, should pray in times of weakness." Around a picture of the resurrection, they might write: "Jesus gives us new life. We feel joy and peace because he was raised from the dead." Give the youngsters an example before they begin, using a picture that is not included in the group.

There are, of course, many other ways to use pictures effectively. Use the techniques that best suit your personality, the needs of your children, and the setting in which you teach. The more you experiment, the more effective and enjoyable your sessions can become both for you and for those you teach.

Summary

- One picture can be worth a thousand words. Both text visuals and other pictures you bring to your sessions can be presented in a variety of ways.
- Textbook visuals might be used as starting points for stories or discussion. Have children name characters, place themselves in the scene, and share thoughts and feelings.
- Ask "behind the scene" questions about pictures that show how the faith can be practiced.
- Other visual aids can be obtained from magazines, newspapers, brochures, calendars, the computer, and even "junk mail." When selecting pictures, see them through the eyes of the children you teach. Study them reflectively, and be prepared to answer questions about them. Choose religious pictures that are reverent and realistic.
- Techniques for using pictures include: picture study, the Name Game, picture story, picture sequence, picture collage, picture challenge, picture report, picture meditation, and picture quiz.
- Use pictures that best suit your personality, the needs of your group, and the setting in which you teach.

Questions for Reflection

How can I make better use of pictures in my religion sessions?

Do I look for pictures other than those provided in my text? Where?

Do I take time to study reflectively the visuals that I use so that I might be ready to answer any questions the children may have?

CHAPTER 9

Making a Connection with Newspapers

*How to use newspapers to demonstrate
the relationship between faith and daily life*

It's difficult to be awake and alert early in the morning as you sit down
with your first cup of coffee and the daily newspaper. But if you're willing to do more than simply skim through the paper, you will find it can
be a useful tool for teaching religion. In their pastoral letter, "To Teach
as Jesus Did," the U.S. bishops said: "New study and effort are needed
to utilize communications media in religious education" (article 96).
When we hear "communications media" we think instinctively of
movies, videotapes, television, computers, and other sophisticated
audio-visual equipment available to us today. However, with all the
modern technological advances we have made in this area, the newspaper has remained one of the most favored, not to mention the least
expensive, means of communication we have in our modern world. As
a tool for presenting your religion lessons, it can serve a valuable purpose as well by illustrating the relationship between the faith we profess
and the faith we live.

Some Examples of How to Use Newspapers
You can utilize newspapers in a number of ways: to introduce a lesson
or topic; to illustrate a particular point you are making in your lesson;

as expressions of views to be challenged; as springboards for discussion; and as material for assignments. While glancing through your paper in the morning, keep your eyes open for articles, columns, and editorials you might use. Here are some examples of what to look for.

Election Time

Around election time, newspapers are filled with articles detailing political promises made by candidates. These might be used as openers or springboards for discussion in lessons on God's promises to Abraham and God's people in the Old Testament, or Jesus' promise to send the Holy Spirit, and his promise to be with us always. They might also be compared to the promises we make at baptism, or the promises made in matrimony.

In the past year or two, the papers have been full of articles about large corporations, CEOs, and other top executives, many of whom have been involved in fraud and injustice. For older children, these articles can spark discussions on responsibility, freedom of choice, morality, and social justice.

Examples of Heroism and Faith

Some newspapers highlight persons in the community who have been outstanding citizens. One article told of a socialite woman in Florida who comforted a young girl stricken with AIDS. While many others were afraid of being in contact with the girl for fear of catching the disease, this woman embraced her with the words: "All you can threaten me with is heaven." Since then, the woman has opened a center for persons who have been abandoned by society and who are trying to turn their lives around. She continues to minister to them in spite of the fact that she had a near-fatal stroke several years ago.

Other articles appear giving examples of great acts of heroism: the courage of the firefighters and policemen who faced grave risks to help those in danger after the destruction of the World Trade Center; those laypersons who sacrificed their lives on Continental Flight 93 in Pennsylvania; and everyone who worked to help the injured at the Pentagon on September 11, 2001. What wonderful examples for showing Christ's presence and action in our world today and for pointing out how we can live our faith courageously and unselfishly. The overwhelming response of generosity toward the victims of September 11 from people all over the nation and the world, and the expressions of prayer that followed, were a perfect example of how God draws good out of evil. The tragedy of September 11 challenges us to examine the Christian forgiveness we profess. As we have heard over and over again, this event has changed us all in significant ways.

The tragedy of the Columbia Space shuttle in February of 2003, was another example of an event which has impacted all of our lives. Children as well as adults were caught up in the sadness that enveloped the nation when the seven heroic astronauts lost their lives on this mission. Previous to their flight, each of them spoke of the awesomeness of the task to which they were called and their eagerness to accomplish their mission in spite of the danger. They saw in their mission the value of something that went beyond themselves. Articles in newspapers quoted young people who spoke of astronauts as their role models—"examples of ambition, integrity, and strength." Children need to be reminded frequently that there are heroes such as these today and that we can learn from their lives.

Articles about the Pope and the Church

The pope and his travels all over the world are subjects of interest even to the secular press. Such articles might be used to demonstrate the world's view of the Church, or serve as an example of how the Church today fulfills Christ's commission to preach to all nations.

The many articles on sexual abuse attributed to our Church's leaders have brought to the forefront the fact that the Church is human as well as divine. Whether we wish it or not, these incidents have made an impact on our children, and we need to allow older children, especially, the chance to express their feelings about them. It is an opportunity to point out to them that our fidelity as Catholics is not dependent on the good actions or bad actions of others, even those who have served as our Church leaders, but on Christ himself and on our faith in him.

Example of Celebrities

Youngsters are always impressed with the opinions of celebrities. From time to time, articles appear that reveal something positive about their lives and their views. Christopher Reeve has impressed us with his positive attitude in the midst of his suffering, and his witness to the fact that a person's spirit gives him great power. Doris Day, in an interview some time ago, spoke of the suffering she had experienced in her life and said: "These experiences are really beautiful." She explained that without them she would not have the strength to face other events in her life. In another article, Aleksandr Solzhenitsyn spoke of what suffering had meant in his life. He described it by saying that a soul "ripens with suffering." He had become so certain of the value of suffering that he could later say, "Bless you, prison, for having been in my life." Examples like these can bring home vividly to your youngsters the meaning of Christ's words: "Blest too are the sorrowing; they shall be consoled" (Mt 5:4) and "Unless the grain of wheat falls to the earth and dies, it remains jut a grain of wheat. But if it dies, it produces much fruit" (Jn 12:24).

Some time ago, I came across an article about Charlie Rich, the country singer. In it he states that, as busy as his musical appearances kept him, he always headed home whenever he got the chance. He said in the article: "I'm a family man. Margaret Ann and the children come first with me. They're worth far more to me than financial gain or fame." This is an example of someone who shows the right priorities, an example that might be used in a lesson on matrimony and family life.

One paper listed "Maxims" of Colin Powell, our Secretary of State. They were maxims that witnessed to a positive and dedicated attitude toward life.

An issue of USA Weekend had an article on Alan Jackson who wrote the moving song "Where Were You When the World Stopped Turning?" about the September 11, 2001 attack on the Twin Towers. When others commented on the greatness of the song, Jackson's response was: "God wrote it, I just held the pencil." What a wonderful response to use when teaching youngsters about the writers of Scripture, and what an inspiration for them to know that celebrities are not afraid to speak of God in public or to give God credit for their gifts. The cover of the newspaper section had printed in very large letters the words: "God, Country, Family," showing the priority that God should have in our lives. The article also included a large, colorful picture of the songwriter that could be used in the lesson.

"Ordinary" People

Ordinary, everyday happenings are also useful as examples. A blackout may be used in connection with a lesson on Jesus as Light of the World. Sports events and all the fanfare connected with them are good openers for a discussion about success and failure in the Christian life. Sometimes articles appear telling of a person who has exhibited honesty in a special way. In a recent letter to the editor a woman wrote that she had driven home from a large mall and left her purse in a shopping cart at one of the stores. When she arrived home, she immediately called the store, and to her complete surprise found out that someone had returned the purse with everything intact. Some time ago I read about two teenagers who found a leather bag with several hundred dollars in it. The teens returned the bag to the owner, saying they had never entertained the slightest thought of keeping it. These are great examples to use in a lesson on honesty.

Recently, an article appeared in a Florida newspaper giving background on a clinical professor of surgery at a university medical school. The surgeon developed kidney cancer fifteen years ago, and in subsequent operations, tumors were removed from his brain, kidney, lungs, skin, and abdomen. Throughout this time, he had the prayers of his Catholic wife, her prayer group, a community of Carmelite nuns, and other friends. The doctor, who overcame all his sickness, acknowledged the wonderful treatments he had received and the great doctors who had worked on him, but added: "Medicine can only do so much—God does the rest." What an inspiring lesson on the power of prayer.

Articles on ecology are common today. One appeared quite some time ago about an eighth grade boy in Winston-Salem, North Carolina, who took action on an ecological problem facing residents there. Peter's Creek, one of the many streams flowing through the city, was being polluted. The young boy walked along the creek, followed pipes to their sources, took notes, and wrote a comprehensive report, which he turned in to the city. He contacted several service station owners and wrote letters to businessmen and others, seeking advice on how to clean up the creek. His report was forwarded to the state office of Water and Air Resources and, at the time of the article, an inspector was expected to visit the site of the pollution. This is a practical example of Christian responsibility and concern for God's world. It is a good illustration of the motto of the Christopher movement: "It is better to light one candle than to curse the darkness."

A Cuban man escaped from his country in a crop-duster plane, with his family and six friends. In flying toward Florida, they found they were running out of fuel and were lost. They wired back to Havana and asked for a Miami-Key West radio frequency but were refused. Two minutes later, they saw a merchant ship in the water, and one of the men said: "God put that boat there." As they flew over the freighter and the plane ditched into the water, the husband and father said: "We prayed to God and we landed." Only one of the refugees died in the landing, and it took forty-five minutes for the freighter to reach them, but the others were all finally taken to ports in Florida, where they were given permission to apply for US residency. After leaving the hospital where they had stayed, the man, his wife, and six-year-old son went directly to pray in the church of St. Mary Star of the Sea in Key West. The article ended with his words: "I had so much faith that I knew we were going to live. I was saying 'Calm down, calm down' to the others." And his wife said: "Thank God we're alive."

Information

I once read an article about the familiar Christmas melody: "The Twelve Days of Christmas" and its possible religious symbolism. According to the article the one partridge represents Jesus Christ; the two turtle doves have been seen as representing the Old and New Testament, Joseph and Mary, or any pair that complement each other; three French hens can be faith, hope, and love, or the gifts of the three wise men; four calling birds are the four gospels, four major Old Testament prophets, or four poetical books from the Old Testament; the five golden rings can be seen as the Bible's first five books, or the five decades of the rosary; six geese-a-laying is supposed to be the six days it took God to create the world; the seven swans-a-swimming suggest the seven sacraments or the seven gifts of the Holy Spirit; eight maids a-milking would be the eight epistles of the New Testament or the eight beatitudes; nine ladies dancing represent the nine fruits of the Holy Spirit or nine choirs of angels; ten lords-a-leaping could be the ten commandments; eleven pipers piping would be the surviving disciples after Christ's resurrection; and finally, twelve drummers drumming suggest the twelve minor prophets of the Old Testament, twelve articles of faith, or the twelve apostles. The article quotes Rev. Neil Roy, assistant professor of theology at the Catholic University of America in Washington, D.C., who says there are many explanations of the song. One of them is that it is a form of teaching called "hedgerow catechism" taught to Catholics in England during the religious persecution that followed the Reformation. This article presents a new and interesting concept to discuss with older children during the Christmas season.

Comics

Even comics can be helpful. Some time ago, *B.C.* by Johnny Hart featured a character sitting beneath a tree, writing that, when everything in life seems to be going wrong, "look down deep inside your heart, and know that God is there." *Ziggy* by Tom Wilson was featured in one issue, gazing at a beautiful sunrise as it was coming over majestic mountains, and saying: "They say God is in the details, but he does a pretty good job with the overall picture, too." The *Peanuts* classic series by Charles Schulz has often featured segments where Scripture is quoted, and *Family Circus* by Bill Keane has frequently presented very Catholic themes. *For Better or For Worse* by Lynn Johnston had a cartoon where the youngest child is talking to her dog and counting something on her fingers and on her toes. The strip ends with her telling Edgar the dog: "Know what, Edgar? Grandma Marian told me to count my blessings, but I don't think I can count that high!" What a beautiful thought to share with children in a lesson on thanksgiving for God's gifts.

Columns and Book Reviews

Each day new examples and illustrations come rolling off the presses of our daily newspapers. Keep your eyes and mind open. Many papers have special sections for youth or for spirituality. Advice columns sometimes have good questions and answers. Columns by persons like Billy Graham ask questions like: "Which is more important—what we believe about God or what kind of life we live?" Hearing another person ask this and listening to a response to it from the newspaper can sometimes have much more of an impact than if you were simply to tell your children the answer to this question. Letters to the editor often suggest topics that are great discussion starters. Even book reviews can be used at times. A review of the book *In God's House* by Bev Cook, listed eleven things for children to remember when they are in God's house. They were very practical suggestions which the author believed would be expressions of reverence for God, and of consideration for others. They would make good discussion starters for children in any grade.

Collect and Organize the Articles

Begin to collect and organize these articles according to topics. Those that strike you most will be the most effective to use with your group. Of course, be sure to utilize not only the secular newspaper but your diocesan or nationwide Catholic newspapers as well. These include many items about local and national events that can be used as examples of Christian living and inspiration, and of the Church's work in the modern world. They can also provide helpful information regarding how you present the faith to your students. An editorial in *The Florida Catholic* (October 24, 2002) gave a new insight into a child's image of God. The writer, Julie McCarty, reported that while discussing with her class how Jesus was like a brother, she met with objections from Angelica, one of her students. Angelica informed her that her uncle was a better image of Jesus "because my uncle spends time with me, taking me fishing and listening to me." On the other hand, her brother "often fought with her and treated her poorly." Angelica further explained that Jesus was on the "same level" as God and her uncle was on the "same level" as her father, whereas her brother was not. This is an important concept to keep in mind when teaching about our relationship with God and with Jesus. Each of the children we teach has relationships that are unique. The notions of God as Father and Jesus as Brother may not always be positive ones. As Ms. McCarty states: "We need many images of God because any one image is limited."

All of these newspaper accounts are easily obtained resources which you can use to deepen children's realization that their faith is related to their everyday life—that in response to the question asked in Billy Graham's column, what we believe and how we live are not two separate things. Faith is not true faith unless it is lived, and we live it in the ordinary circumstances of our everyday life. If we believe this and want our youngsters to believe it, we can't afford to pass up any opportunity to demonstrate it. So, as you drink that first cup of coffee in the morning, pay attention to the possibilities available in that daily newspaper lying on your kitchen table.

Summary
- Newspapers can help us illustrate the relationship between the faith we profess and the faith we live.
- Newspaper articles can be used to introduce a lesson or topic, to illustrate a particular point you are making in your lesson, as an expression of views to be challenged, as a springboard for discussion, and as material for assignments.
- Some examples of articles that might be used are those around election time; articles about freedom of choice or social justice; those that highlight persons in the community, or great acts of heroism, or travels of the pope; those on difficult questions to be faced by the Church, the opinions of celebrities, or examples of honesty, prayer, and faith; those with other religious themes and illustrations of everyday happenings.
- Other portions of the newspaper that might be utilized are sections on youth, spirituality, advice columns, religion columns, letters to the editor, book reviews, and even comics.
- Diocesan and national Catholic newspapers should also be used, as they include examples of Christian living and inspiration.

Questions for Reflection
Am I aware, as I read the daily newspaper, of connections between the news and my faith life?
Have I ever been inspired to live my faith more fully by something I read in the newspaper?
How can I use newspapers to help the children I teach understand this important connection between faith and daily life?

CHAPTER 10

Don't Ignore the Board!

How to make good use of an often neglected teaching tool

We used to call them blackboards, but there aren't many black ones left any more. They come in green, or brown, or sometimes even blue. In many instances they have been replaced by white, or dry, eraser boards, with markers instead of chalk for persons allergic to chalk dust. But whatever shape or form it comes in, the board will always be a "magical" tool for catechists.

Advantage of Using a Board

Chalkboards and dry-eraser boards have a two-fold appeal. They help to capture the children's attention and to focus it on the material you are teaching. They can also bring life and movement to your teaching. The dimension of movement that a chalkboard can add to storytelling is especially important to children growing up in a world that never stands still. There are moments, of course, when a lesson may call for a "still" illustration, for example when using a picture for reinforcement, review, prayer, or meditation, but most often lessons should be alive and active, always on the move. Chalkboard visualization can be one way of achieving this.

If you are fortunate enough to have a meeting area with a board you can use, here are some important points to keep in mind.

Be sure your board is cleaned off ahead of time. If it is a chalkboard, remove the dust from the chalk tray, and have the chalk and eraser handy for use. If your chalkboard stretches across the room, keep chalk and an eraser at either end.

When writing on the board, do it at the eye level of the children you are teaching rather than your own. If you have a movable board, bring it as close as possible to the group without impairing the view of those who sit along the sides.

Don't overcrowd the board with words and pictures. Like any other visual aid, simplicity and clarity are most important. If you have several groupings of words or drawings and there is not enough distance between them, separate them by lines or boxes so that the children can clearly see the distinctions.

If you are using chalk rather than markers, use the soft variety as it is more easily read from a distance. If you have difficulty with the dust and must resort to hard chalk, be sure to press firmly on the chalk when writing, so as to make it clearly visible from a distance. Why not test out the visibility of your writing before class begins by standing in the back of the room to examine it? The same applies to the use of dry erase markers. Often, they do not write heavily enough to be seen at a distance, so if you are using them with a dry erase board, test these out as well.

Illustrating Stories on the Board

One of the ways to bring movement to your lesson is by using the board to illustrate a story. You don't have to be an artist to do this. If you can draw circles, squares, rectangles, or lines, you can narrate almost any story with stick figures. When you are illustrating biblical stories, however, it is more reverent to use a symbol for Jesus, rather than attempt to draw a figure of him. A cross, a chi rho, or a crown might be appropriate, and is easily drawn. It also provides an opportunity to explain the symbols to the class.

In general, if your art is amateur and brings out a chuckle from the class now and then, that's not necessarily bad. Often we wrongly equate seriousness with reverence, but a little lightness in our lessons from time to time can be beneficial. It can help the children realize that their faith is something that should bring joy into their lives.

With younger children, using colored chalk is also helpful. In a lesson on the story of the prodigal son for second graders, I once attempted to illustrate the story on the chalkboard with stick figures, using colored chalk. I did all the figures themselves in white or yellow, but drew a palm tree in brown and green, and the little pigs with circular bodies in pink chalk. The children laughed at the little pigs, but it made an impression on them and helped them remember the story weeks later. As you present a story in this way, be sure you do not turn your back on the class while you are drawing. Try to do one scene at a time as you relate it, turning sideways as you draw and looking back at the class from time to time. Occasionally, invite the children to come to the board and write a response to a question or draw a picture.

Other Ways of Using the Board

Whenever you are giving the children lists—like the sacraments, the commandments, or the beatitudes—write these out on the board, or have the children take turns writing them. If the children already have them listed in their textbook, let them read them out to you or to the children writing them on the board. This reinforces what they have already read.

When teaching a definition, write it out completely and have the children read it together. Then erase a few words of the definition and have them read it again, supplying the missing words. Continue to erase the words and have the children read the entire definition each time, until it is completely erased. By that time, the children should be able to say it from memory.

Use the board to display large pictures, maps, diagrams, or flash cards you are using in your lesson. Use stick tack or masking tape to attach them. Write comments around the pictures or maps. Have any faith words you want the children to remember written in a corner of the board where you can refer to them at the proper time. Have any assignment you wish the children to do listed on the board when they come into the room, so they can copy it before the lesson begins. When using religious crossword puzzles, rather than give out individual copies, draw a large one on the board and have the whole group work it out together. Use the board to list the words to songs you are teaching. Children, especially in the middle grades, enjoy competitive games. If you form the group into teams for games, choose captains for the teams and invite them to come to the board to keep score for their team.

Storyboards or Felt Boards

A different kind of board is the storyboard or felt board. These can be purchased at an arts or crafts store, or you can make your own. Tack two large pieces of felt to a large (at least 3' x 5'), thick piece of cardboard: a light blue piece for the sky and a green piece for the grass/ground. Trace and cut out figures and mount them on felt: Jesus, the apostles, other biblical characters, the saints, animals, trees, mountains, and so on. Prop the board up where it will be at eye level for the children. With a little rubbing, the figures will stick to the felt, and you can tell stories by moving them around on your board.

There is nothing sadder than to walk into a classroom of active but distracted boys and girls and to see a board that is completely empty. Don't let yours go to waste. If you are teaching in a room that is used by another teacher and find the board always in use, try to arrange it so you have at least a portion of it freed for use on the day you teach. You'll find that the more you use it, the more exciting the lesson can become for you and the more enjoyable for those you teach.

Summary

- Boards—whether chalkboards, white or dry erase boards, or story boards—have a two-fold appeal: they help capture the children's attention and focus it on the material you are teaching, and they bring life and movement to your teaching.
- Some important points to keep in mind when using a board are: if it is a chalkboard, be sure it is cleaned off, and chalk and eraser are ready; write at the children's eye level; don't overcrowd the board with words and pictures; use soft chalk or press firmly so that your writing can be seen by the entire class.
- When drawing figures for stories, use symbols for Jesus rather than trying to draw a figure of him. Use colored chalk with young children, and remember that if your art brings forth a chuckle from the class, this is not necessarily bad. When writing on the board, try to turn sideways and look back at the class from time to time. When possible, invite the children to come to the board.
- Use a storyboard made with a felt background and figures to tell Bible stories and the lives of the saints.

- Use the board for listing things; teaching definitions; displaying large pictures, maps, diagrams, or flash cards; writing faith words and assignments; drawing crossword puzzles; writing words to songs; and playing games.
- If you find your board always in use, try to arrange to have at least a portion of it freed for your class use. The more you use the board, the more exciting the lesson can be for you and the more enjoyable for those you teach.

Questions for Reflection

Do I consider the board a valuable teaching tool? Why or why not?

What use have I made of the board in my religion lessons?

How can I make my lessons more effective and enjoyable by using a board?

CHAPTER 11

Using Audiovisuals

*How to create interest in your religion lesson
through the use of audiovisuals*

Are visual aids really necessary or important to use in faith formation sessions? *The General Directory for Catechesis* states: "The very evangelization of modern culture depends to a great extent on the influence of the media." No one can deny the powerful effect modern media has had on the children we teach. As catechists then, we need to utilize the more popular forms of this media, such as videos, DVDs, TV programs, films, CDs and cassettes.

Videos/DVDs

If your parish has the equipment needed, there is a plethora of wonderful videos available telling Bible stories and the lives of the saints for all ages. Other videos have stories about prayer, the Mass, the sacraments, or the Church seasons. Still others illustrate real-life situations in which young teens find themselves. These can be obtained through your parish, your Diocesan Religious Education Office, or sometimes even the public library. Using these videos brings a change of pace into your religion sessions and adds depth to the presentation of Christian witness, sacraments, Scripture, and other faith topics.

TV Programs

Even if you don't have access to video equipment for your religion sessions, you can find much helpful material for your lessons in many of the programs offered on television, both for older and younger children. Whether the programs explicitly teach values and morals or not, you can use examples from them to discuss what the children should or should not do in certain situations. *Recess,* for example, which airs on Saturdays, presents situations in which grade school children successfully face and solve their moral dilemmas. In *Lizzie McGuire*, a popular show for preteens, the young star and her friends have to make real-life decisions about friends, family, responsibility, and so on.

Other programs that are popular with youngsters may promote lifestyles or messages not consistent with Christian morals. With older children, use panel discussions or surveys to help them realize why these messages are not consistent and to make their own judgments about the programs. Have them rewrite the outcome of one of the episodes to illustrate a Christian message or point of view.

Material from news programs can be used in the same way as newspaper articles. Images on television often impress children in a way that printed articles cannot. If a significant local or national event is aired on TV, the children may want to discuss it with you. Of course, care must be taken when the event has a very tragic or emotional impact.

Films

Whether in the theater or on television, films are another form of media that have a big influence on youngsters. How many of them have seen *Harry Potter*, the more recent episodes of *Star Wars*, and *The Prince of Egypt*, to mention just a few? These as well as other recent films contain material for discussion starters about the Bible, faith, life after death, "magic," and more. As you watch these films, try to think of faith-related questions they might bring to children's minds, for future reference in a lesson.

CDs

Both younger and older children have their favorite music CDs. Some of these can be used effectively for musical backgrounds for prayer or for teaching. You may want to invite older youngsters to bring in any CDs they think fit the theme of something they have learned in their religion session, or even have them write their own lyrics to the songs.

Some of the popular songs have negative messages or run counter to Christian values. These can be used as discussion starters as well, to help your youngsters realize what kinds of messages and lifestyle the music is promoting, so they can make informed decisions about their choices.

Cassettes

Another means that is often overlooked today is the cassette recorder. Yet it, too, is a practical and helpful tool that can be used in a variety of ways. My sixth grade youngsters and I came to realize that it could play an instructive and interesting part in our religion lessons. One day I pulled one off the shelf, dusted it off, and turned it on. Since that day, we have used the recorder again and again in our different sessions. It has provided a new means of participation, fortified important points in the lesson, and helped greatly in making practical applications.

Taping Bible Stories

Occasionally, instead of telling or reading a Scripture story, try taping it ahead of time and playing it at the appropriate point in your lesson. You can add a great deal of drama to it in this way, and if you wish, add sound effects and some quiet music in the background. If there is dialogue between persons in the Scripture story, as for example, in the story of the rich young man (Lk 18:18–23) or the Samaritan woman (Jn 4:4–42), have others take part in the dialogue, one acting as narrator, and the others as characters in the story.

Pantomime

Younger children, especially pre-school, kindergarten, and first graders, love to pantomime. If you are using a taped story with them, you might want to have them pantomime the actions of the characters as they are mentioned in the story. Some scripture stories that lend themselves well to this are: the wedding feast at Cana (Jn 2:1–11), the multiplication of the loaves and fishes (Jn 6:1–13), the parable of the prodigal son (Lk 15:11–32), and Jesus blessing the children (Mt 19:13–15).

Dialoguing About Practical Applications

We all know that being formed in Christ and living the faith, not just learning it, is our ultimate goal in teaching religion. Yet so often, we get caught up in the presentation of the material and have little time left to discuss practical applications: how can I live my life today in a truly Christ-like way? Perhaps this is because we feel it is difficult to make this part of the lesson interesting. Cassettes can be helpful here, too.

Record on a cassette some brief examples of situations that the young-sters can analyze as applications of the lesson. For example, in a lesson on community, you might tape a conversation between two girls discussing someone who has just registered in their school. If possible, show the group a picture of two girls, suggesting that they are the two who are speaking. The girls' conversation might be a positive one, showing their willingness to extend friendship to the newcomer as Jesus would, and make her a part of the group. Or it might be negative, showing that they are exclusive and not open to newcomers—a situation that your group can challenge. Give names to the girls to make it more personal and believable, but be sure not to use the names of any of the children in your group. Prepare questions for the group to answer after they have listened to the tape. For example: Do you think these girls (give names) are acting in a Christ-like way? Are they building up a spirit of community by their attitude? Why or why not? What do you think Jesus might think about their conversation? Do you think that most boys and girls your age feel this way about newcomers? What do you think Jesus might tell these girls to do? What could you do to build up a spirit of community in this situation? If the conversation you recorded was a negative one, you might want to have the youngsters write a more positive, community-minded response they think would meet with Jesus' approval.

Ending a Story

Another approach can be to use a recorder for taping unfinished stories. Tape a situation in which a boy or girl is left with a decision that involves honesty, truthfulness, friendship, concern, sharing, or whatev-er the main theme of your lesson is. Let the children write or suggest their own endings to the story, telling which decision they think would be Christ-like for the person to make. Have the group evaluate the deci-sions and choose which they think is the best one and why. Their answers often provide valuable insights into their attitudes and person-alities. After teaching a Scripture story about Jesus, as a review, you might also want to play a recording of the story, stopping it before the end, and having the children finish the story in their own words.

Introducing Topics

Cassettes can also be helpful for introducing topics you might want the group to write about. For example, you might record a newspaper article, letter to an editor, or editorial on a topic related to your religion lesson and ask the children to write a response. Chapter 9 on using the newspaper suggests some ideas for doing this.

Teaching Songs

Many religion programs have music tapes available to accompany their lessons. These are especially useful with younger children. Make use of those provided for you. But if you have none, why not create some songs of your own, using well known children's melodies. Here are three examples of some you might try:

Lesson:	We are all God's children, no matter what color our skin is.
Melody:	The Farmer in the Dell
Words:	Oh, God made us all
	Oh, God made us all,
	White, brown, red
	Or yellow skin,
	God loves us all.

Lesson:	We want to be like Jesus.
Melody:	Jingle Bells (chorus only)
Words:	Jesus came to be like us
	On that first Christmas day.
	Jesus, make us just like you
	In all we do or say.
	(Repeat)

Lesson:	Jesus teaches us how to live and share.
Melody:	Twinkle, Twinkle, Little Star
Words:	Jesus, show us how to live,
	Jesus, teach us how to give.
	All we think, and say, and do,
	We will give them all to you.
	Jesus, show us how to live,
	Jesus, teach us how to give.

Play the song on tape for the children. Then have them sing it along with the tape. Little children are always delighted at hearing their own voices recorded, so you may also want to tape them singing it together as a group.

Be Creative

There are, of course, many other uses for cassettes. Use them to tape descriptions of biblical characters and have the class identify them. If you are teaching older children, assign one to conduct a survey on some topic you have discussed and play it back for the group the following week. Encourage the boys and girls to bring in any tapes of songs they know of which might reinforce what they have learned.

However you decide to use any of these audiovisual aids, you will find that they can be effective tools for teaching if used properly, and can add a spark of new interest to your presentation.

Summary

- Videos and DVDs provide an alternate and engaging way of presenting Bible stories, the lives of the saints, faith topics, and themes for discussion.
- Television and films can be used as discussion starters; some of them address real questions of faith and life. News programs can be used in somewhat the same way as newspaper articles.
- CDs can be used as background music for prayer or teaching,
- The cassette recorder can also provide new means of student participation, fortify many important points in your lesson, and can help greatly in making practical applications of the lesson.

Questions for Reflection

Have I ever made use of audiovisuals in any of my religion lessons? Which ones worked best with my group?

Have I ever used a television program or film as part of my religion lesson, either to give an example or to begin a discussion? Why or why not?

How can an audiovisual help me achieve the goal of my lesson?

What can I do to make better, more effective use of these teaching aids?

CHAPTER 12

Are You Asking the Right Questions?

How to help children think more deeply about their faith by asking the right kind of questions

"I like having Mrs. Hendricks for religion class," my niece informed me one day. "Why?" I asked, curious to know what this fifth grade catechist's special appeal might be. I expected a pat answer like: "She lets us have fun," or "She tells us funny stories in class." Instead, my niece said: "When we ask her questions, she doesn't answer right away. She makes us figure it out for ourselves."

I reflected on my niece's surprising response, and began to realize that her catechist was using one of the same teaching techniques that Jesus had used. When a lawyer came to him asking what he must do to gain eternal life, Jesus responded by asking another question: "What is written in the law?" After answering his own question, the lawyer was still not satisfied. "And who is my neighbor?" he asked next. Jesus did not answer him directly. Instead he responded with a story that provided more food for thought, the story of the good Samaritan (Lk 10:30–37). When Nicodemus, the Pharisee, came to Jesus at night filled with questions about salvation, Jesus spoke to him in figurative language, encouraging him as a "teacher in Israel" to think things out for himself (Jn 3:1–21). Even when an answer to

Pilate's question, "What have you done?" might have saved his life, Jesus did not answer Pilate directly. Instead, he aroused Pilate's curiosity further by speaking of a kingdom not of this world (Jn 18:35–38).

Ask Thought-Provoking Questions

For children growing up in our modern world, the black and white answers provided to us in the past are not sufficient. Children today need to be guided by us in discovering the truth for themselves as far as possible. We need to help them reflect deeply on their faith so they might gain confidence in their own ability to find answers to life's questions. We catechists are not helping them to achieve these goals if we always give them direct answers and don't provoke them to think things out for themselves. Of course, there are exceptions. There certainly are moments when children need simple explanations, and there are children whose mental abilities are not yet developed enough for complex reflection. But it is much easier to fall into the trap of answering everything directly than to guide children toward answers. The technique of helping children find answers for themselves is not something that is achieved in a year or two, but we can begin even in the lower grades to sow the seeds for this growth. Asking good questions is one way to do it.

Here are some examples of thought-provoking questions taken from a contemporary religion series.

First grade	Why do you think Jesus wants us to be fair to everyone?
	Can you think of something Jesus has taught you?
	Why do people sometimes need to work together?
Second grade	How can we stay close to Jesus?
	Why do you think we need to love other people?
	What does this season of new life (spring) tell us about God?
Third grade	How will you try to keep growing in your faith?
	How can Jesus help you when you worry? (During Advent) What do you think our Church is waiting and hoping for?

Fourth grade	Why do you think we should care about the lives of others? How do you know when you have made good decisions? What are some of the best ways to get ready for Christmas?
Fifth grade	How does God want you to treat people who are different from you? What do you think it means to be a person of hope? How does remembering Jesus make a difference in your life now?
Sixth grade	Why does being a prophet take courage? What qualities do people need to be good leaders in our faith community? How can we become better listeners to God in our life?
Seventh and Eighth grade	What difference should the communion of saints make in our lives as Catholics? Why is it important to know that the Bible is the Church's book? Why do you think some people look for happiness in sex, power, money, music, alcohol, or drugs?

(Reprinted with permission from the *Coming to Faith* series, 1999 and the *Faith and Witness* series, 1998, Keystone Editions, Wm. H. Sadlier Company, NY)

Questions like these are very different from fact questions like "Who is Jesus' mother?" or "How many commandments did God give Moses?" or "When did Jesus die on the cross?" While there are certain facts the children should be required to know, we can't let their knowledge stop there. We need to help them delve into the deeper meanings and reasons for their faith if we want that faith to mature.

Help Younger Children Mature in Their Thinking

Most young children think in concrete terms. This was brought home graphically to me when I read *The Family Circus* comic strip by Bill Keane one day. It showed a picture of dad telling his wife that he was going somewhere that was "just a hop, a skip, and a jump away." His little son is shown picturing his dad, hopping, skipping, and jumping. The young daughter also hears her mom on the phone saying: "I've been down in the dumps all day." The little girl pictures her mother sitting in the middle of a junkyard. Because young children think this way, we try to avoid asking questions that are too abstract. But, on the other hand, it doesn't hurt to promote growth in thinking by helping even younger children stretch a little beyond the merely concrete level. So in first grade, for example, a question like "What is the Mass?" may be a little too abstract for them, but you might show a picture of a family going into church and ask, "Why do you go to church on Sunday?" While you would not ask a second grade child, "How can you be an evangelizer?" you might ask instead, "How can you help your friends know more about Jesus?"

Make Your Questions Visual

Instead of just asking questions, appeal to the children's sense of sight as well when you are questioning. For example, draw a stick figure on the chalkboard or on a chart. Give the stick figure person a name, or ask the class to name him or her. Then have the "person" drawn ask the question for you. With children in the middle grades, you might draw a "balloon" like the ones in comic strips, and print the questions inside, or cut out pictures of boys and girls from magazines or newspapers, give them names to personalize them, and then have these cutout "persons" ask the questions for you. With a picture of a young boy you could say: "Jack wants to know: What can I do to help my friend Mike get to know Jesus better?" Or with a picture of a girl, you might say: "Susan asks: How can I explain to Karen what the Eucharist is?" It is a simple technique, but it is surprising how much more it captures the attention of the youngsters than merely asking the question yourself. Finally, don't neglect the ever popular question box. Make up questions ahead of time and print them on colorful pieces of paper. Fold them and put them in a box with a large question mark printed on its top. Then invite the children to take turns drawing and answering a question.

The Next Step

Knowing the importance of asking good questions is not enough. The next step is helping children develop thoughtful questions of their own. One catechist I know composes test questions from those the children have asked her in their religion sessions. I remember, too, that one of my college professors tested our knowledge of his subject by asking us to write questions rather than answers on the topic. The implication was that if we could ask a good question about a subject, we really knew it well.

We can use children's questions as an effective introduction to new material. A week or two before teaching new material, invite them to write out any questions they have about the topic and put these in your question box. Then print them on a large chart or in a corner of the chalkboard and leave them in front of the group until the day the lesson is to be taught. It's amazing how curious they can be and how ready they are to listen for answers to their own questions. Compliment all the children who submit questions, but especially those who have asked truly thought-provoking ones.

Whichever techniques we choose, we should be convinced of the importance of asking good questions. If we can help our children to think things out for themselves, we will be giving them the best possible preparation for living a committed Christian life. And the good news is, good questions can help catechists grow in faith as well.

Summary

- Rather than answering questions directly, Jesus helped people to think things out for themselves.
- Children need to be guided in discovering the truth for themselves and reflecting deeply on it.
- Even though young children think more in concrete than abstract terms, we should help them grow in their thinking.
- Make your questions "visible" with stick figure drawings, "balloon" questions, pictures, and question boxes.
- Help children develop the ability to ask good questions as well as give good answers.
- Helping children think things out for themselves is the best possible

preparation for living a committed Christian life, and can help you grow in faith as well.

Questions for Reflection

What can I learn from Jesus' method of asking and answering questions?

Do I take time to prepare good questions for my group?

How can I make my questions more "visual"?

What have I done to help the children I teach think more deeply about their faith?

CHAPTER 13

Making Use of the Computer
How to use your computer
as an effective resource for your religion lessons

Computer is one of those words that can cause responses from one extreme to the other. Some may respond with an "Ugh!" and others with a "Wow!" Whichever your response might be, if you have even an elementary knowledge of the computer, don't overlook it as a resource for your religion lessons.

A Word Processor and Art Source
As a word processor, your computer can be an invaluable aid in outlining the important ideas you want to cover in your lesson each week, for typing up information or notes for those you teach, and also for enlarging and printing out key words you want the children to remember. The clip art section on most computers allows you to print out pictures of persons, scenes, and symbols you might find useful in making charts or simply to illustrate a lesson.

A Source for Catholic Information
If you have access to the Internet, there are innumerable opportunities for helpful information in almost any field imaginable. Here are just a few of the websites available for Catholic teaching:
www.alapadre.net
www.usccb.org/laity
www.catholicweb.com

www.catholic-extension.org
www.bellarmine.lmu.edu/fjust/
www.VATICAN.VA
www.staycatholic.com
www.OnceCatholic.org
www.holyfam.com
www.pauline.org

A Source for Stories

As we read the newspaper each day and listen to both world and local news, we sometimes wonder if there are any really good, inspirational stories available that we might share with the children in our groups. We have already seen that there are such stories in the newspaper if we take time to look for them. Bt what about the Internet? Like our regular postal service mail, our e-mail can often be bombarded with an enormous supply of "junk mail." But frequently there are also stories that are not only appropriate for our groups, but that can be really uplifting for them.

United Flight 93. Just within the past year, for example, I received an e-mail about Todd Beamer, the passenger on United Flight 93 who led the charge against the terrorists on September 11, 2001. The email quoted his words: "I don't think we're going to get out of this thing. I'm going to have to go out on faith." The e-mail spoke of his faith in Jesus Christ and said that "more than once, he cried out for his Savior." Beamer called the GTE Customer Center in Oakbrook, Illinois. He told supervisor Lisa Jefferson about the hijacking and what they were going to do. Then he asked her to pray with him the Our Father. He added, "Jesus, help me." All the passengers recited together the psalm, "The Lord is my Shepherd" before Todd's final words: "Let's roll."

If you are on the Internet, you must have received countless stories, articles, and illustrations about the terrible events of September 11, 2001. Many of these were printed out and shared by catechists with youngsters in the upper grades as background for discussions on good and evil, on Christian faith and prayer, on God's presence and protection, and on the need for forgiveness. They provided concrete and very challenging examples of what Jesus really asks us to do when he says: "My command to you is: love your enemies, pray for your persecutors" (Mt 5:44). The events of September 11th also brought about an intense interest in learning more about the faith of others and a desire to understand and accept those whose beliefs might differ from our own. Again, Jesus' words to his apostle John were recalled: "Anyone who is not against us is with us" (Mk 9:40).

God Finds Tommy. Another e-mail told a true story about John Powell, a professor at Loyola University in Chicago who wrote about Tommy, a student in his theology class. Tommy claimed to be an atheist, and as John Powell stated, "He constantly objected to, smirked at, or whined about the possibility of an unconditionally loving Father/God." After finishing the course, Tommy cynically asked his teacher, "Do you think I'll ever find God?" And his teacher replied, "No." Tommy's response was, "Oh, I thought that was the product you were pushing." As Tommy was leaving the classroom, John Powell called out to him, "Tommy! I don't think you'll ever find him, but I am absolutely certain that he will find you!"

Some time afterwards, Tommy returned to see his old teacher—this time the young man had terminal lung cancer. He had only a few weeks to live, and he was only twenty-four years old. Tommy proceeded to tell his former professor how he had tried to reach out to God but could not feel his presence, and how he had given up. He remembered that John Powell had told his class it would be sad to go through life without telling those we love of our feelings. So Tommy went to his family and expressed his love to all of them, and received their love in return. It was then, he said, that *God found him,* as John Powell had said he would. Powell asked Tommy if he would be willing to tell his story during one of the class sessions, and Tommy agreed. However, before the time came, Tommy called to say that he didn't think he would make it. So he asked John Powell to tell his story to the students and to the whole world.

The Diver's Prayer. Another story entitled "The Diver" told about a young man who had been raised as an atheist and who was training as a diver for the Olympics. Although his Christian friend spoke to him often about his faith, he didn't pay much attention to him.

One night he went into an indoor pool at the college to practice his diving. The lights were off, but he thought he could see well enough because of the skylights and the bright moon out that night. He climbed to the highest diving board and stood backwards on the board to prepare for his dive. As he stretched his arms out to his sides, he noticed that his shadow on the wall was in the shape of a cross. Instead of diving, he knelt down and asked God to come into his life. As he stood up again, the maintenance man came in and turned on the lights. The pool had been drained dry for repairs! Had he jumped, he might have been killed or crippled for life. His prayer had saved him.

Billy's Dream. One story I received on the Internet illustrated the Christian love and concern of a group of firefighters in Phoenix, Arizona. A young mother had a six-year-old son who was dying of leukemia. She asked her son Billy if he had ever dreamed about what he would like to do with his life. Billy's response was: "Mommy, I always wanted to be a fireman when I grew up." The mother went to the local fire department and spoke to a fireman named Bob to ask if her son might ride on the back of their firetruck one day.

Fireman Bob's heart was so moved that he responded in an even more generous way. First, the firefighters had a uniform made for Billy, with a real fire-hat, not a toy one, with the emblem of the Phoenix Fire Department on it, a yellow slicker like the one they wore, and rubber boots. They made Billy an honorary fireman for a day, invited him to have lunch with them at the fire house, and then let Billy go out with them on all three calls for that day. He rode on the fire truck, in the paramedics van, and even in the fire chief's car. They let Billy help steer the truck back to the fire station when the day ended. Billy was also videotaped for the local news.

Having his dream come true filled Billy with such joy that he lived three months longer than had been expected. When it seemed like the end was near, the nurse at the hospital called to ask if one of the firemen could be with Billy when he died. Again, Fireman Bob responded with an outpouring of Christian love for this little boy. He came with a whole group of firefighters in the truck, asked the nurse to let people know there was no fire, and requested that she open Billy's window. The fire truck came to the hospital with its siren running so Billy could hear it. When they arrived at the hospital, sixteen firefighters climbed a ladder to Billy's window and entered it. With his mother's permission, they all hugged and held him and told him how much he was loved. Billy looked up at the fire chief and asked, "Chief, am I really a fireman now?" The Chief's response was, "Billy, you are, and the Head Chief, Jesus, is holding your hand." Billy responded, "I know, he's been holding my hand all day, and the angels have been singing." And Billy closed his eyes for the last time.

There are many other true inspirational stories that can be found daily on the Internet. These can be valuable motivators to those you teach. Don't pass up the opportunity to share some of these stories with them.

Sources of Other Helpful Information

There is no end to the variety of information that you can garner from the Internet to use in your religion sessions. Here are some other examples.

I learned from one source the origin of the tune "Taps," which is played at military funerals, and the words which remind us that God is near. During the Civil War, a Union soldier had a son who had gone south to study music. Unknown to his father, he had enlisted in the Confederate army. During the battle at Harrison's Landing, Virginia, the father heard the moans of a soldier who had been severely wounded. The father, who was a captain, did not know if the man was a Union or Confederate soldier but risked his life to rescue him. When he lit a candle to look at the man, he was shocked to discover that it was his own son. The following day, the captain asked permission to give his son a military burial with an army band playing a funeral dirge. The request for the funeral was granted, but the army band denied. However, out of respect for the father, he was allowed to have one musician play. He chose a bugler, and gave him a piece of paper with a series of musical notes he had found in his son's pocket. It was the melody which we now know as "Taps", and these are the words:

Day is done, Gone the sun, From the lakes, From the hills, From the sky. All is well, Safely rest, God is nigh.

Fading light Dims the sight, And a star Gems the sky, Gleaming bright. From afar, Drawing nigh, Falls the night.

Thanks and praise For our days, 'Neath the sun, 'Neath the stars, 'Neath the sky. As we go, This we know, God is nigh.

Perhaps this little story will remind your youngsters that "God is nigh" and that we should give "thanks and praise" for all "our days" in this world.

I received a copy of a "School Prayer" which attempted to show the contradiction in outlawing prayer in public school, when we are a nation "under God." The prayer stated that students are allowed to have purple, orange, or green hair, they can pierce their "noses, tongues, and cheeks" and yet had to meditate "in silence alone" because "God's Name is prohibited by the state." The prayer describes other contradictions in the rulings, and would be an interesting springboard for discussion in a class on prayer, on true freedom, or on faith.

Lastly, another e-mail provided the legend of the candy cane in a story and a poem. It was first created by a candy maker who wanted to make a kind of candy at Christmas time that would be a witness to the Christian faith. He started with white candy to symbolize the virgin birth and the sinless nature of Jesus. He made it hard, to symbolize the foundation of the Church on a "rock" and on the solid promise of God. If you look at the cane, you can see it looks like a staff—that of the Good Shepherd—and if you turn the candy cane upside down you will see that it is made in the shape of a J to stand for Jesus. The candy maker added three narrow red stripes to stand for Jesus' scourging, and a wider red stripe to stand for the blood Jesus shed for us on the cross (Legend of the Candy Cane).

One year, at a Christmas party given for the children in our religious education program, each one received a candy cane with a copy of this legend printed on a green piece of construction paper. The cane, with a red bow around it, was taped to the paper. The parents and catechists were as pleased with the gift as the children were.

Motivational Phrases and Advice

Sometimes simple phrases, like proverbs and advice given by someone over the Internet, can make more of an impression on those we teach than simply hearing the words from us. Here are some examples I have found helpful:

"I've learned that you shouldn't go through life with a catcher's mitt on both hands. You need to be able to throw something back." (Maya Angelou)

"Anger is only one letter short of danger." And "He who loses money, loses much. He who loses a friend, loses much more. He who loses faith, loses all." (Eleanor Roosevelt)

"The shortest distance between a problem and a solution is the distance between your knees and the floor. The one who kneels to the Lord can stand up to anything." and "You are richer today if you have laughed, given or forgiven." (Food for Thought and Soul)

This is only a small indication of the valuable help you can receive for your religion classes from the Internet. On saintoftheday.com, you can receive inspiration and information about lives of the saints. You can search the Internet for knowledge of other famous persons, and for almost any religious topic you might be covering. Invite your older children to do searches on specific topics that pertain to their faith. You will be surprised at their eagerness to do this. So, if your computer draws an "ugh" response from you now, change it to a "wow" by using it as a truly helpful resource tool for your religion sessions.

Summary

- The computer can be a helpful resource for your religion sessions.
- As a word processor, the computer can aid you in outlining ideas you want to cover, typing information or notes for your group, printing out key words or clip art for charts or for illustrating some point you are making.
- The Internet can be a source of Catholic information, of inspirational stories, of letters to God, of lives of the saints and other famous persons, of other helpful information, and of motivational phrases and advice.

Questions for Reflection

Do I view the computer as a help or a deterrent to my religion class? Why?

How can I become more alert to what is helpful for my religion class on the Internet?

What specific topics will I research on the Internet for my group this year?

CHAPTER 14

Prayer and Prayerfulness

*How to instill prayerfulness in the children you teach,
and help them learn their prayers as well*

It is not surprising that the apostles requested of Jesus one day, "Lord, teach us to pray." They had been with him for some time and had watched him at prayer. They had seen, too, the prayerful way he approached people and things, and it made them want to pray as he did. As catechists we are called to teach prayers and, even more importantly, to instill in those we teach an attitude of prayerfulness. Both are necessary: prayers, because as the children grow in their faith life, the prayers they learn in childhood can become like anchors in their lives, especially in times of pain and hardship; prayerfulness, because it will help them to constantly maintain a sense of God's presence in their lives and will give them the strength and peace they need to live their Christian life in today's world.

Setting Up a Prayer Corner

If your meeting room does not have a prayer corner, arrange to make a portable one to set up and use each week as a prayer space. Attach a picture of Jesus to a flannelboard, decorate it, and place it on the chalkboard ledge. Or bring in a small carton, cover it with a white cloth, and arrange a Bible and a candle on it. Your setup need not be elaborate. It is simply a point of focus around which to gather the children. Look at your textbook carefully to see which prayers or teachings about prayer it includes, and use the suggested prayer approaches it offers. If these are not appropriate for your group, design some prayer moments of your own, and be sure to make time to include them in your lesson.

Taking Time to Wonder

Wonder is the seed from which prayerfulness grows. You will see it often in a young child's eyes or even in the eyes of an older youngster as he or she is exposed to the beauty of the woods or of outer space, for example. But the seed of wonder needs to be nourished. Your expression of wonder when teaching about God can help to deepen your children's own sense of God's awesomeness. Does this sense of wonder come through to them when you teach about creation, about God's great love as expressed in the Scriptures, about the great gift of Jesus and his compassionate love for all people? Do you approach Jesus' gift of himself in the Eucharist, the gift of his life on the cross, the glory of his resurrection, and the sending of the Holy Spirit with wonder and praise? Does your own prayerfulness help the children to know and love Jesus better?

As you teach about these many expressions of God's great love, let the children see and sense your wonder. Then, take a prayer "breather," a few moments for them to close their eyes, to feel the wonder of God's love, and to whisper a prayer of praise. It need not be a long prayer. A few words like "My God, I praise and love you" are enough, or "God, I think you're wonderful!" You might want to have the children pray a line or a phrase from one of the many psalms of praise in the Bible, or if their textbook offers a prayer, take time to pray it as well.

Spontaneous Prayer

Instead of always beginning class with a traditional prayer, lead the children occasionally in a spontaneous prayer from your heart. From time to time, offer older children the opportunity of leading the group in a prayer from the heart. You may also wish to lead your group in an intercessory prayer like that used in the Mass and let them add their requests. This was an especially helpful type of prayer at the time of crisis our nation underwent in the aftermath of September 11, 2001, and again in February of 2003.

Writing a Letter to God

If you have ever written a letter to a friend, you know that it is probably one of the easiest kinds of letters to write. You feel free to open your heart and express your innermost feelings to a friend. Take a few moments at the end of a religion session to let the children write a letter to God or to Jesus their friend, or even to one of the saints they may have learned about. Encourage them to write spontaneously about anything they want to share, or suggest that they write about what they have learned that day and how they feel about it. If some children wish, they may share their letters, but do not make this a requirement as it might keep them from freely expressing their feelings. If you have a prayer corner with a picture of Jesus or one of the saints, you may wish to have them fold their letters and place them in front of the picture.

Guided Meditation

Children can be taught simply to meditate at a very early age. If you have an especially beautiful picture, like a picture of Jesus blessing the children, you can post this at the front of the room and lead the children in a few minutes of guided meditation. Post the picture where all may see it easily. Then invite the children to quiet their minds and hearts and look at the picture. Lead them with these words: "Pretend that you are there in that group of children. Look right into Jesus' eyes and see his kindness there. What would you like to say to Jesus? (Allow a few quiet moments.) Did you hear Jesus say anything back to you? If you did, think about that quietly for a few minutes. (Allow more quiet time.) Talk to Jesus quietly in your own heart now; tell him how you feel when you are close to him. Tell him in your own words how much you love him, and how you will show your love for him today."

With older children you might wish to read very slowly a short Scripture reading, allowing time at appropriate places for them to reflect quietly. For example you might read this part of Jesus' discourse at the Last Supper slowly and with feeling, pausing for a few moments after each sentence: "Do not let your hearts be troubled. You have faith in God; have faith also in me. In my Father's house there are many dwelling places. If there were not, would I have told you that I am going to prepare a place for you? And if I go and prepare a place for you, I will come back again and take you to myself, so that where I am you also may be" (Jn 14:1–3).

Singing and Choral Reading

Singing a prayer is a wonderful way to praise God, and one that appeals to young children in particular. Many textbooks contain songs that you might use, with melodies adapted from music the children are familiar with, for example, "The Farmer in the Dell," "Three Blind Mice," or "If You're Happy and You Know It." From time to time you may want to use the parish hymnals to sing a hymn the children have heard at Mass. Older children sometimes enjoy doing choral reading of a prayer, with background music playing softly. Mass prayers like the Gloria or the Our Father lend themselves beautifully to this type of expression.

Drawing a Picture

Children love drawing pictures for their parents. I have yet to see a home with young children that doesn't have a supply of pictures hanging on the refrigerator door. Invite the children to draw a picture for God, their loving Father/Mother, telling God about themselves, something they have learned, or praising God for something beautiful they have seen. Let them share these if they wish. Then post them around the room so they can look at them from time to time.

Prayer in Motion

Explain to the children that sometimes the gestures we make with our bodies can be words "in motion." Demonstrate some examples: waving our hand says "hello" or "goodbye," a smile says "I'm happy," a hug says, "I love you," a bowed head says, "I'm sad" or "I'm sorry." Have the children contribute examples of their own. Question them about what the action of holding hands during the Our Father at Mass means. Then lead them in praying a prayer such as the Glory Be to the Father, Our Father, Hail Mary, Act of Contrition, or a simple Morning Offering prayer, using motions with each phrase. You may wish to have the children suggest some motions for a prayer, or choose the motions you think would be most expressive for them. Here is a suggestion for a simple Morning Offering prayer you might use with motions. Practice it with the children until they know it well enough to pray it, following your guidance. Encourage them to share it at home with their parents and siblings.

My God (hands folded)
I offer you today (hands uplifted)
all I shall think (hands on forehead)
or do (hands extended)
or say. (hands on lips, then extended outward)
Uniting it (arms crossed)
with what was done (hands extended)
on earth (hands joined in half circle)
by Jesus Christ, (hands folded, heads bowed)
your Son. (hands uplifted)
Amen. (hands joined together)

Celebrating Liturgical Seasons

With intermediate and older children, especially, you will want to incorporate prayer forms that fit well into the liturgical seasons, for example the "O Antiphons" during Advent, an Act of Contrition during Lent, a decade of the Rosary during the months of October or May, a portion of the Litany of the Saints on All Saints Day, or a sung Alleluia during Eastertime. Older children also relate well to prayerfully listening to or reciting psalms which express wonder and awe, thanksgiving, praise, or contrition. Scriptural phrases from both the Old and New Testaments can lend themselves to moments of quiet reflection. For example, during the Christmas season, these words from Isaiah would be an appropriate prayer: "For a child is born to us, a son is given us; upon his shoulder dominion rests. They name him Wonder-Counselor, God-Hero, Father Forever, Prince of Peace. His dominion is vast and forever peaceful" (9:5–6). And for Holy Week, use some of the powerful sentiments Jesus expresses in these words from his prayer to the Father at the Last Supper: "I pray not only for them (the apostles), but also for those who will believe in me through their word, so that they may all be one, as you, Father, are in me and I in you, that they also may be one in us, that the world may believe that you sent me" (Jn 17:20–21). Let the youngsters stand quietly in a circle, holding hands, while you prayerfully read these words to them. Or post a beautiful picture of Jesus at the Last Supper, invite the group to "place themselves there" next to Jesus. After viewing the picture for a few moments, suggest that they close their eyes and try to feel Jesus' presence next to them as you read his words. End with a few moments of silence so they can reflect quietly on Jesus' prayer.

Learning Prayers Correctly

When teaching prayers, take time to go over the words carefully, one phrase at a time, making sure the children are hearing the words correctly. Some children have been heard praying, "Hail Mary, full of grapes," and "O my God, I am hardly sorry for having offended you." Use the chalkboard or flash cards to explain the meaning of the phrases so that the children can actually see the words, especially those that can be easily misinterpreted. Take time to review the prayers with them. The Missing Lines Game (see Chapter 17) is a fun way to help them do this. Encourage parents, as well, to go over the prayers with their children, and to take time to pray some of the traditional Catholic prayers with them at home.

Incorporate at least some form of prayer into each class you teach, either as part of your lesson, or before or after the presentation. Pray both spontaneous and the familiar traditional prayers with attention and reverence. Remember that prayerfulness, like appreciation for our faith, is something that is more "caught" than taught. It is your own prayerfulness that will be the most powerful factor in helping those you teach to love prayer and to pray often.

Summary

- As catechists, we are called to teach prayers and, even more importantly, to instill an attitude of prayerfulness in those we teach. Prayers can become like anchors in children's lives, especially in times of pain and hardship. Prayerfulness will help the children maintain a sense of God's presence in their lives and give them the strength and peace they need to live a Christian life in today's world.
- It is helpful to have a prayer corner as a point of focus around which the children can gather.
- Some suggested ways to teach prayer and instill prayerfulness are: taking time to wonder, spontaneous prayer, writing a letter to God, guided meditation, singing and choral reading, drawing a picture, prayer in motion, and celebrating liturgical seasons.

- Some type of prayer should be incorporated into each session, either as part of the religion lesson, or before or after your presentation. Take time to go over words and phrases in prayers so that the children understand their meaning.
- Prayerfulness, like appreciation for our faith, is something that is more "caught" than taught. Your own prayerfulness will be the most powerful factor in helping those you teach to love prayer and to pray often.

Questions for Reflection

Do I take some time for prayer in each religion class I teach?

Do I reflect a spirit of prayerfulness to the children I teach?

How can I best help the children "catch" this spirit of prayerfulness?

How can I help them learn the Church's traditional prayers?

CHAPTER 15

Presenting the Saints

*How to introduce children to the saints
and motivate them to imitate the saints' lives*

Faith formation programs over the years have undergone profound change. To the simple explanation of the catechism we have added Bible stories, life experiences, liturgical teaching, and prayer celebrations. We have incorporated into our religion lessons activities, games, music, art, and at times, even dance—all in order to make religious education more interesting and engaging. Yet it will always remain true that nothing motivates us more than example, not only of the people around us but also of those who have gone before us. This is where presenting the saints to our youngsters comes in. The way you present the lives of these great heroes and heroines of God can greatly influence how children will live out their faith.

The Saints Are Human Like Us
We need to help children see that the saints are not only heroic figures to be admired; they are also persons whose heroism they can follow. We can imitate the saints because, like us, they have experienced human weakness, yet despite that weakness they have kept their faith, hope, and love alive. Living a saintly life is possible for us because the saints have shown us that God never demands more of a person than he or she can give. Saints are not strangers to us; they are friends who understand and support us in our struggles because they have experienced

similar ones. They are not persons who have run away from life; they are men and women who have lived life as fully as possible. Some of them did it in simple, unpretentious ways, like St. Thérèse of the Child Jesus, who lived a quiet, hidden life as a Carmelite sister from the time she was fifteen. She performed no extraordinary deeds in her life but simply tried at all times to be the most loving person she could be. She called this her "little way." She tells in her autobiography of how irritated she became when the sister who sat in front of her distracted her at prayer by rattling her rosary beads. Rather than express her irritation, Therese tried to be extra kind to her. Little acts of heroism like this are something children can imitate.

Try to impress on those you teach that there is no great distance between the saints and us, only an appearance of distance created by time. We can be sure the family and friends of Thomas More, for example, no more thought of him as a saint than we do the many good persons with whom we rub elbows everyday, those who live heroically in our midst and who will become the saints of tomorrow. Closeness has a way of dimming our vision.

Be casual in your approach when you present the saints to children. Avoid the temptation of being overly dramatic and using spectacular imagery. If you have a sense of "at-home-ness" with the saints, it will be transmitted to your youngsters. Be creative in the way you introduce the saints. The following are some approaches you can take.

Growing Up in God

Show a picture of an infant baptism and the baptism of an adult. Explain how each of us is born into the spiritual life and called to grow in it throughout our lifetime. Have the children suggest ways they can do this: through prayer, celebrating the sacraments, doing good works, and so forth. Help them see the saints as regular persons who grew in the life of holiness they received in baptism. Talk about some ways in which they did this, using examples from their lives. Be sure to emphasize the ordinary things that they did extraordinarily well, rather than the spectacular aspects of their lives that children cannot imitate. For example, Joseph, the foster-father of Jesus, never worked miracles in his lifetime. He grew in holiness by living out the life of a husband and father, working each day to support his family, praying together with them, doing acts of kindness for his neighbors, and accepting all that God sent into his life—but doing it all with great love.

Using Our Gifts

Talk with your group about the experience of giving gifts. Ask them if they have ever given someone a gift that was not used. How did it make them feel? We show our appreciation for a gift when we use it. Give them some examples from your own life of things you have received which you have used over and over again, and explain how much that pleased the persons who gave them. With older children, you may wish to write on the chalkboard these words from Vatican II: "The Holy Spirit gives to the faithful special gifts. Each believer has the right and duty to use them in the church and in the world for the good of mankind and for the building up of the church" (Article 3, Document on the Laity). Discuss this statement with them. Talk about the fact that God has given each person special gifts. Some seem more dramatic than others but all of them are important to the building up of Christ's body. Read St. Paul's words from 1 Corinthians 12:20–22: "There are indeed, many different members, but one body. The eye cannot say to the hand, 'I do not need you,' any more than the head can say to the feet,' I do not need you.' Even those members of the body which seem less important are in fact indispensable." Help the youngsters see that each of us has a gift that is important to God, to the Church, to the world, and that it is by using this gift well that we grow in holiness, like the saints.

Tell or read to the group the story of one of the saints, pointing out the special gifts he or she used for God's work. For example, St. Paul used his gift of preaching to teach others about Jesus. St. Thomas Aquinas used his intelligence to write about and teach the truths of our faith. St. Monica used her gift of prayer to bring about the conversion of Augustine, her son. St. Ignatius Loyola used his gift of leadership to organize a group of men who became the priests of the Society of Jesus. St. Francis of Assisi loved the poor. He gave all his possessions to them and began his Order of Franciscans to reach out to those in need. St. Elizabeth Seton used her knowledge to start an order of sisters to teach the young. Point out that these persons became saints not because of the unique gifts they received, but because of how well they used their gifts for the good of others and for the "building up of the church."

You may wish to relate this to the parable of the silver pieces (Mt 25: 14–30). Each servant was asked to use and be responsible only for what was given him. Have the children reflect quietly on the gifts God has given each of them. Ask them to choose one gift that they think they can best develop in the service of others. Lead them in a prayer, offering this gift to God and asking God's help to develop it to the best of their ability. Have them pray also to any saint you have presented to them, asking the saint's help to develop these gifts.

Reflecting the Lord

Talk with the girls and boys about sunlight and the phenomenon of the rainbow which appears when the sun shines after a rain shower. Explain to them how all the varied colors are contained in the light itself, and how sunlight is a combination of colors. Compare this to Christ and the saints. Christ called himself the "Light of the World" (John 9:5). He possesses all the virtue and all the goodness that it is possible for anyone to have. He is our principal exemplar. But just as all colors are contained in light, each of the saints is like a color, reflecting in some special way one or more of the virtues of Christ, the Light. We honor them because they are reflections of Christ. Some saints were examples of his love for the poor and afflicted, others of his obedience, some of his mercy to his enemies, still others of his prayer. Have the group list some of the saints with whom they are familiar and the virtues they see emphasized in their lives.

Invite the youngsters to reflect quietly on their own lives and to think of some virtue they possess which reflects Jesus in some way. Let them draw a picture or write a poem or a few sentences to show how they might grow in that virtue; then lead them in a prayer, asking God's help to grow in holiness.

Younger Saints to Imitate

Tell the children stories about younger saints around their own age—like St. Tarcisius, an early Christian, who carried communion to those in prison and sick at home. He was a teenager, attacked by a gang because he was a Christian. Tell them about Maria Goretti, another teenager, who was murdered in an attempted rape because she refused to give in to her attacker. St. Bernadette of Lourdes was the daughter of a poor family but was privileged with several appearances of Our Lady. She was an example of purity and courage, remaining faithful to God's wishes, rather than giving in to peer pressure. St. John Berchmans went to study for the priesthood as a Jesuit at the age of nine. He never became a priest because he died of a serious illness at a young age. But John was a common sense saint. One day while he was playing a game with a companion, he was asked what he would like to be doing when it came time for him to die. Everyone expected him to say, "Oh, I'd like to be in chapel, or serving Mass, or receiving communion." Instead John told them he would like to be doing just what he was doing at that moment. John realized that it doesn't matter whether we're doing something great or small. As long as it is what God wants, we are always ready to see God. St. Dominic Savio, a pupil of St. John Bosco, was a peacemaker among the boys at his school. He often put himself at risk, intervening in fights and persuading the other boys to make peace with each other. St. Katharine Drexel was raised in a Catholic family and as a youngster helped her mother in her good works for the poor.

Some Suggested Activities

When your religion session occurs on a saint's feast, make a few short remarks about the saint and open your class with a prayer to him or her. Encourage the boys and girls to learn as much as they can about the saints through reading or on the Internet. You can find a brief summary about the saint of each day at this Internet address: http://saintfora-day.com. Some may want to look up their own patron saint or the patron saint of the parish.

Show an occasional video on the life of a saint, or read a portion of a story without completing it to arouse your youngsters' interest. Besides the many books available on the saints, there are also trading cards on the saints, similar to the sports trading cards that children love to collect. The cards contain the birth and death dates, an historical overview of the saint's accomplishments, canonization information, and a prayer to the saint. Have the children each choose one and read the information to the group, or assign one to each child for a report the following week. Some catechists have found it helpful to let the youngsters make puppets of their favorite saints and use the puppets to tell their story. Others have had girls and boys dress as their favorite saint and dramatize an incident from that saint's life. This would be especially appropriate around the feast of All Saints. (See Resources section at the end of this book.)

Remember that nothing motivates like example, and the saints offer us a marvelous array of examples to choose from. Presenting the lives of these holy persons to your youngsters will help them realize that there is a hero or heroine inside themselves and that they, too, can live holy lives.

Summary
- The way we present the saints can greatly influence how children will live out their faith.
- Saints are not only heroic figures to be admired; they are also persons whose heroism we can follow. We can imitate them because like us, they have experienced human weakness, yet despite this weakness they have kept their faith, hope, and love alive. They are not strangers but friends who understand and support us. There is no great distance between us and the saints.
- Be casual in your approach when teaching about the saints. Avoid the temptation to be overly dramatic and use spectacular imagery.
- Some approaches to teaching about the saints are themes such as: growing up in God, using the gifts God gave us, reflecting the Lord.
- Introduce the children to saints their own age, like St. Tarcisius, St. Maria Goretti, St. Bernadette of Lourdes, St. John Berchmans, St. Dominic Savio, St. Katharine Drexel, and St. Thérèse of Lisieux.
- Presenting the lives of these holy people to your youngsters will help them realize there is a hero or heroine inside themselves and that they, too, can lead holy lives.

Questions for Reflection
Am I a true witness to the good news of Jesus?

How much of an influence have the saints had in my own life?

How can I present the saints in a way that will motivate youngsters to become holy?

CHAPTER 16

The Dilemma of Discipline

*How to create an atmosphere of discipline
and help develop self-discipline in those you teach*

What thoughts and feelings come to you when you hear the word discipline? Does it bring to your mind and heart flashbacks of harsh commands, of knuckles being hit with a ruler, of angry corrections, or punishments of various kinds? Most of us have these negative images of what discipline really means. If you were to look up the definition in the dictionary, you would probably find that most definitions support this impression. Because of this, we often feel faced with a dilemma as we ask ourselves, "How can I present the faith to those I teach in a loving, pleasant way, and yet maintain discipline?" The word discipline, we know, is actually taken from the root word for disciple or follower. It is a wholesome and necessary quality in everyone's personal life, especially in that of a follower of Christ.

Discipline is a Part of What We Should Teach
Discipline is important to catechists, not only because learning won't happen without it, but because it should really be a part of the youngster's learning. A disciplined person is in control of his or her life, and this self-control is the necessary foundation for growth in the Christian life. Jesus the Master Teacher said, "The spirit is willing, but nature is weak" (Mk 14:38). Nature often pulls us in many directions, and without discipline our lives are not truly free. If we think of discipline as a

quality that frees us to live as followers of Christ, instead of something that limits us, it takes on a whole new meaning, especially in a country that so values freedom. The kind of discipline that we want to foster in our children is not the kind that lasts only while they are in a learning situation, but one that continues into their everyday life. But how can we accomplish this?

Teach Discipline By Your Own Example

You are the greatest determining factor in maintaining discipline in the group. Pope Paul VI once said: "Modern man listens more willingly to witnesses than to teachers and if he does listen to teachers, it is because they are witnesses" (Pope Paul VI to Council of Laity, October 2, 1974). This is true of children as well. The very first day you stand before them, the children will be observing your manner of dealing with them. They may not be able to define the quality that you demonstrate in your teaching situation, but they sense easily if you are a disciplined person, in control of yourself and your surroundings. If you are a disciplined person, you do not have to be harsh with the children. Rather, they will see by the manner in which you deal with them, that you really care about them and enjoy being with them. They will also see that you are there because you have something important to share with them and that you are eager to do this in as pleasant a way as possible.

Some Helpful Ways to Maintain Discipline

Here are some suggestions that you may find helpful in creating an atmosphere of discipline with your group.

Your Manner

Get to know the children as individuals. Children, like adults, thrive on attention. Call each one by name, and learn which ones need your attention the most. If you give them the attention they want in a positive way, they may not feel it necessary to seek it in a negative way. Help them also see that you like them as well as love them.

Combine a warm manner with a professional one. Help the children see that you are a confident, disciplined, mature person, ready and eager to share your faith with them.

Develop a sense of respect in your group. Your respect for every child will help them respect you and one another. Listen carefully to what each one has to say and try to understand her or his comments. Sarcasm and ridicule have no place in any type of learning situation but especially not in a religion session. Let the boys and girls see that you expect the best from each one, and that you do not have anyone pegged as a troublemaker, even if he or she had this reputation in other classes. If you expect trouble, you will probably find it. Instead, give every child the opportunity to start over.

Maintain a balanced sense of humor in your relationship with the children, and respond well to their humor when they express it. Years ago, when teachers of religion taught catechism questions and answers, I recall asking Lionel to respond to the question: "What must we do to get to heaven?" The catechism answer was: "To get to heaven, we must know, love, and serve God." Lionel's wide-eyed and smiling response was: "Be good, be quiet, and behave." I thought that was an excellent interpretation from Lionel, who was not the most attentive child in the class. I responded with a smile and let him know I agreed.

Your Presentation

Be well prepared. Know your lesson well and have your teaching materials at hand so that your presentation runs smoothly. Start your lesson on time, know where you are going, and keep the lesson active and moving. Nothing promotes discipline problems more than a catechist's hesitation or a child's boredom.

Don't be afraid to admit that you do not know an answer or that you have made a mistake. You are human, and the children know it. Assure them that you will do your best to find an answer for them.

Your Situation

Insist on an orderly procedure from the very beginning. Order does not mean rigidity. It means moving things along as smoothly as possible, without unnecessary interruptions. Having a few simple rules which everyone can follow will help. Be sure they are necessary and in the general interest of the whole group. Make sure that each child knows and understands the rules. Print them on the chalkboard or on a chart where they can be seen at all times. Be consistent. Don't suppress a child's action one day and permit it the next. Be fair. Treat everyone equally, as far as possible, taking individual personalities and circumstances into consideration.

Learn the right moment to assert yourself. Children know that there is a certain line beyond which they should not pass. Sometimes, when a youngster is causing a disturbance, becoming very quiet and giving him or her a penetrating look (what one university professor calls his "laser" look) or moving closer to the child, is enough to stop it.

Know when to overlook something that was done unintentionally or without malice. Not every transgression is of equal importance. Don't overreact to disturbances. There may even be times when it is wiser to ignore one.

Developing Discipline in the Children

Your manner, your presentation, and the way you handle your situation with the group will greatly determine how they respond during your presentation. But how can you help the children develop their own self-discipline?

Motivating them with stories of the saints and of other heroic persons can help. The saints could not have achieved the greatness they did without discipline. Point out this fact as you relate stories like the ones mentioned in Chapter 15 about St. Thérèse of the Child Jesus, St. Tarcisius, St. Maria Goretti, St. Bernadette of Lourdes, and other saints. More contemporary witnesses include Mother Teresa of Calcutta, St. Maximilian Kolbe, Kateri Tekakwitha, Martin Luther King, Jr., and others with whom they may be familiar. Discuss with the children the discipline needed for someone to train to be an astronaut, a football or basketball player, a policeman, fireman, doctor or nurse, a musician or an actor, and so on.

Another custom which I have found motivates children to practice discipline is that of Advent and lenten practices. During the liturgical season of Advent, we encourage the children to prepare their hearts for Jesus' coming by performing acts which entail some sacrifice. The following are some examples.

To prepare my heart for Jesus' coming, I will be kind to someone at school who looks sad or alone.

To prepare my heart for Jesus' coming, I will eat everything I am served at home or in school without complaining, even if I don't like it.

To prepare my heart for Jesus' coming, I will study my religion lesson instead of watching TV after supper.

To prepare my heart for Jesus' coming, I will pay extra attention in all my classes at school.

To prepare my heart for Jesus' coming, I will watch my sister's (or brother's) favorite TV show instead of mine.

To prepare my heart for Jesus' coming, I will invite someone who is not popular at school to play with me.

To prepare my heart for Jesus' coming, I will take five minutes each night before I go to sleep, to think quietly about God's love in sending Jesus to us, and to thank God for this.

To prepare my heart for Jesus' coming, I will drink water instead of soda with my meals this week.

To prepare my heart for Jesus' coming, I will try to do something helpful for my mom or dad today.

During the lenten season, we encourage the children to offer sacrifices in union with Jesus' suffering on the cross, and to show our gratitude for all that he suffered for us. Here are some examples of what the children can do.

To show my love for Jesus, I will thank him each night in my prayers for offering his life for me.

To show Jesus that I want to be strong as he was, I will stand up for what is right, even if I know others will make fun of me.

To show Jesus that I want to become a loving person like he was, I will go out of my way to help someone I don't like.

To show Jesus my love during this Lent, I will study my religion lessons carefully and share what I have learned with someone else.

To show Jesus I am grateful for the sacrifice he made of his life, I will share my favorite snack with someone I don't really like.

To show Jesus I am grateful for all he has done for me, I will take time to read about him from the Bible this week.

To show Jesus I am grateful for what he suffered, I will try to do my chores at home more cheerfully, without complaining.

To show Jesus I want to be like him, I will be especially respectful to my parents and teachers.

To thank Jesus for all the suffering he endured for me, I will keep my room at home neat and clean this week, without being asked.

You will be more familiar with practices that would be helpful for your group. Create some of your own. The practices can be typed or written on small slips of paper which the children draw from a box each week before or after class. You may also want to make a chart on which the children can place a flower or a star around a picture of the nativity for each practice they complete during Advent. For Lent they could place small crosses around a crucifix or a picture of Jesus. The simple sacrifices the children make can help instill in them the beginnings of self-discipline. Younger children, especially, love these Advent and lenten practices, and older children find them challenging. I have always been pleasantly surprised at the eagerness with which they choose them each week, and how proud they are at viewing their charts covered with flowers or stars.

Hopefully, you will find some of these suggestions appropriate for your group. Remember that each child is an individual, and each group is unique. Take time to reflect on the different personalities of the children you teach, as well as on your own, and adapt the suggestions to them. You may come to find that it is possible to keep a balance between a joyful presentation of the good news and maintaining discipline in your teaching situation. It is no longer a dilemma.

Summary

- Discipline is a wholesome and necessary quality in everyone's life, especially for a follower of Christ.
- Discipline is important to catechists, not only because learning won't happen without it, but because it should really be a part of the children's learning experience.
- If we think of discipline as a quality that frees us to live as followers of Christ, instead of something that limits us, it takes on a whole new meaning.
- The kind of discipline we want to foster in our children is one that continues into their everyday lives.

- You are the greatest determining factor in maintaining discipline in your teaching situation. Your manner should be attentive, warm yet professional, and respectful. Your presentation should be well prepared and your lesson engaging. Don't be afraid to admit you don't know an answer or that you have made a mistake. Your situation in the religion class should be orderly and guided by a few simple rules.
- Know when and how to assert yourself.
- To help children develop self-discipline, tell stories of the saints and of contemporary heroes, highlighting the discipline in their lives. Use Advent and lenten practices to encourage them to make small sacrifices in their daily lives.
- Reflect on the personalities of the children you teach and on your own, and adapt any suggestions to them. It is possible to keep a balance between a joyful presentation of the good news and maintaining discipline in your teaching situation.

Questions for Reflection

In what ways am I a disciplined person?

How can I grow in self-discipline?

How can I better help those I teach grow in self-discipline?

What can I do to improve discipline in my teaching situation?

CHAPTER 17

Adding Those Finishing Touches
How to include those important last steps
in your religion lesson

One time, when I was working as a DRE in a parish, I received a call from a parent. She was upset because her fourth grade son couldn't explain what he had learned in his weekly religion class. Unfortunately, this is a common frustration for parents, and they tend to wonder what we are teaching their children. This incident motivated me to talk with the catechists about the importance of finishing up their lessons with activities that summarize and help children to remember what was taught. When children come only once a week, it is difficult for them to remember what was covered unless we take time to review and pull it all together for them. If the children you teach answer "nothing" or "I don't know" when asked what they learned in your class, perhaps you need to examine whether or not you are putting "finishing touches" on your religion lessons.

The Importance of Adding Finishing Touches
Finishing touches are important in everything we do: decorating a cake, polishing a car, landscaping a home, or furnishing a room. Teaching religion is no different. In fact, the finishing touches in a religion lesson are probably the most important steps of all. Most of us begin our sessions with enthusiasm. We carefully prepare to engage our youngsters in what we will be teaching by using some examples from their every-

day lives. We enter into the presentation of the lesson, making it as vivid as possible, using the Bible as a resource, remembering to make use of audio visual aids, keeping the lesson moving, and then suddenly, we are surprised to see that it's time to stop! We never seem to get to the final steps where we help the children to assimilate, organize, and express what we have taught.

Most teacher manuals today provide an outline for those final steps of the religion lesson, but unless we schedule in the time to use them, they are left out. The result is that children are unable to express what they have learned, and parents, after questioning their children, are left wondering if they have learned anything at all. Perhaps we feel that by the last ten minutes of our session the children are too tired for a recap or review. This is not true if we continue to be enthusiastic about our presentation to the very end. If you think the children have become rest-less, try some quick activity to call them back to attention. With little ones, you can give them a minute to stand up and stretch. With older students, ask them to sit up in their seats and "put on their thinking caps." Then introduce them quickly to some activity that will tie things together for them. Here are some suggestions for making this part of the lesson interesting while still reinforcing what they have learned in their minds and hearts.

A Talking Sentence Game

With very young children, if your religion lesson does not provide a faith summary, find two or three sentences that summarize the important points you have covered in your lesson. Line up some children in the front of the room (one for each word in a sentence) and whisper a word of the sentence in each child's ear, in the correct order. Instruct the children to say their word loud and clearly, one after the other, at a signal from you. Tell those who are seated to listen carefully to each word so they can repeat it afterwards. Signal the children with a bell, a clap, or a nod of the head, and have them speak their words in order. Then have each child in the group step forward and say their word again, but this time, invite the entire class to say their word with them, so that the whole group repeats the sentence together. Make any additional comments about it that you wish, and then have the next group come up and repeat the process with their sentence. Repeat the procedure until all the material has been covered.

Next draw stick figures or use a picture representing parents and invite the children in each "sentence group" to explain something about their sentence to these "parents." For example, a sentence in second or third grade might read: "Jesus gives us the gift of himself in holy communion." The children might add that gifts are something for which we are grateful, or they might tell of Jesus' great love in giving us himself, or talk about ways in which they can give themselves as gifts to Jesus and to others. When first using this technique, you may need to help the children phrase their thoughts by asking questions. But once they have become accustomed to this procedure, encourage them to add comments on their own whenever possible, so that they become accustomed to expressing what they have learned in their own words.

A Picture Study

If you have used pictures or charts in your lesson, line them up on the chalkboard ledge and invite the children to come forward, choose a picture, and tell what they remember about it. Or you might hold up the pictures one at a time, and ask the children to write a sentence about each one. Give them an example to help them get started. When all are finished, have them share their sentences. List these on the board as they are read, and then have the whole class read them together. If you have not used additional visual aids in the presentation of your lesson, have the children use the pictures in their textbook.

A Grab Bag

Divide the group into two teams, for example, "angels" and "saints." Have slips of paper ready with key words used in your lesson. Place them in a small brown paper bag and invite one "angel" and one "saint" to come forward and draw out a slip of paper. Let each one call on someone on her or his team to write a sentence on the board, using the word drawn, or with younger children, have them give a sentence for you to write on the board. When all have finished, have the class read the sentences together. Add any important points they may have left out.

A Jesus Diary or Journal

This activity works best with children in fourth grade and up. Display any pictures you have used in a particular lesson and write on the chalkboard any key words or concepts that you have covered. Give each child several sheets of writing paper, and invite them to begin writing a daily diary addressed to Jesus, telling him about what they have learned in their class today. Suggest that they use the pictures and key words or concepts as guides. Give each youngster a sheet of folded construction paper to make a cover for their diary. You may wish to have them use this technique for an entire unit's lessons. Older students may prefer to call their book a Jesus Journal. Since a diary or a journal is private, do not require that they read theirs to the class. They may wish to share it with you. If so, use it as a means to help them grow spiritually, but respect their confidentiality.

A Crossword Puzzle Game
This activity should be prepared ahead of time. Make a list of key words you have used in the lesson and create a simple crossword puzzle using those words. A scrabble board and tiles can help you prepare this. Draw the puzzle grid on the chalkboard or on a chart, with the clues listed beside it. Read the clues one at a time. Invite a child who thinks he or she knows the answer to come up and write it on the grid. Ask the class to decide if the answer is correct. If it is not, have another child come up and add the correct word. When the puzzle is completed, assign a word to each one in the class and have them tell something (other than the clue) they remember learning about that word. If you prefer, you may have the puzzle printed out for each child and let them work out the answers at their desks. Then go over the entire puzzle with them before having them tell what they remember about their assigned word.

Drawing the Lesson
Younger children, especially, enjoy expressing themselves in art. Pass out drawing paper and invite the children to draw a picture of the most important thing they learned in the day's lesson. When all are finished, have them share their pictures and invite others to add anything they wish to each child's explanation.

Writing a Letter
Ask the children to pretend a new child will be joining their group the next week. Give the child a name. Have them write a letter, explaining to this child what they have learned in the day's religion lesson. Let them illustrate their letters with drawings if they wish. Then have them share

the letters and vote on which ones they think best explain the material.

Filling in the Blanks Race

Divide the chalkboard or a sheet of posterboard in half vertically. On each side, write summary sentences describing points from the religion session you want the youngsters to remember, including how they are to live what they have learned. Omit some of the key words in each sentence and replace them with blank lines. Have the children form two lines, one in front of each side of the chalkboard or chart. At a signal, let them come up, one at a time, fill in a missing word, and then pass the chalk or marker to the next person in line. If the next person sees that the word is wrong, he or she may change it and then add another as well. Be sure there is a blank for each child to fill. Whichever side finishes first, with all the right answers, wins the race. Have this team read the summary together, each adding her or his word out loud. Let the whole group read the summary a second time to reinforce the ideas.

Class Religion Scrapbook or Mural

If you are teaching older youngsters, and time permits at the end of the year, you may want to have them make a group Faith Formation Scrapbook, covering all the important topics they have learned. Divide the scrapbook into sections, one for each unit you have covered, and give each section a title. Have each youngster choose one of the sections and suggest that he or she draw a picture, make a small poster, or write a poem or short essay to illustrate something learned about that section. Ask each one to sign his or her name to their work. Allow time when all are finished to share their contributions. Then put them all together into the scrapbook. You may want to display this at a parent meeting, or in the parish hall.

You could also do this as a mural if you have the wall space to display their work.

Adding these finishing touches to your religion lessons and your year's work will add variety and interest to your sessions and help your children integrate what they have learned in a pleasant and effective way. Let them see the need for living what they believe by instilling in them a sense of pride in their faith and a desire to share it with others.

Summary

- Finishing touches in a religion lesson are probably the most important steps of all. Because children come to our religion classes only once a week, it is difficult for them to remember what was covered unless we take time to review and pull it all together for them. Unless we schedule time for the final steps of the lesson, these summaries are often left out.

- Some activities that might be used as final steps to help your youngsters integrate what they have learned are: A Talking Sentence Game, A Picture Study, A Grab Bag, A Jesus Diary or Journal, A Crossword Puzzle Game, Drawing the Lesson, Writing a Letter, Filling in the Blanks Race, and a Faith Formation Scrapbook.

- Adding these finishing touches to your lessons and to your year's work will give variety and interest and help your children to integrate what they have learned in a pleasant and effective way.

- Let the children see the need for living what they believe by instilling in them a sense of pride in their faith and a desire to share it with others.

Questions for Reflection

How often do I run out of time before adding the finishing touches to my religion lesson?

How can I make certain the children are integrating the material I teach?

How can I better plan my lesson so as to allow time for this at the end of each session?

CHAPTER 18

Making Repetition Enjoyable

*How to reinforce in new and creative ways
what you have already taught*

"Repetition" is not a popular word today because it suggests boredom. "New," on the other hand, has a magical and exciting sound, and the way we devour products, ideas, and even TV shows labeled "new" proves it. This fact can put catechists in another dilemma. Repetition has always been considered an essential element in the learning process. Yet we want our lessons to be new and appealing for the children. What procedure should we follow, then? Should we sacrifice a vivid presentation in favor of repetition, or should we ignore repeating important material in order to make our lesson more attractive? Do we really need to make a choice? Is it possible to accomplish the best of each of these alternatives?

Rethinking Repetition

As catechists, our first step should be to change our way of perceiving repetition. Think of it more as a reinforcement or strengthening of what the children have already learned. If we think of it positively, it will influence their attitude concerning it. You might want to compare it to tightening a screw. When you first join two pieces of wood together with a screw, you simply insert it in the right position. But it won't accomplish its purpose unless it is tightened enough to hold the pieces of wood together securely. Repetition "tightens" the knowledge and understanding that our youngsters acquire so that it can become a permanent part of their lives. If it is clear and secure in their minds, they will more easily relate future knowledge to it. You will also be reinforcing a Christian way of living and acting which goes beyond formulas. The need for this reinforcement can challenge us to think up new ways of presenting old material, or of going further into something that has already been learned. Be imaginative and playful in your approach to it and you will find it as enjoyable as the children will. Here are some ideas that have proved successful and that may suggest new approaches to you.

The Missing-Lines Game
This simple technique is helpful in reviewing definitions to be learned. It is especially appealing to younger children, but I have used it effectively with fifth and sixth graders as well. In one fifth grade text, the following definition was given for the gift of faith: Faith is a virtue that enables us to trust and believe in God, to accept what God has revealed, and to live according to God's will.

Write the definition in sections on the chalkboard, and have the youngsters read it together. Then erase a word or a phrase at a time, not necessarily in order, and have them try to repeat the complete definition after each erasure until the entire definition is gone. The youngsters enjoy the challenge of trying to remember the missing words, and by the time they have repeated the definition five or six times, they should know it well. This game may be used to review definitions of the sacraments, names of the apostles, literary forms in the Bible, the commandments, the spiritual and corporal works of mercy, the beatitudes, prayers, and so on.

Teacher For A Day
Intermediate grade youngsters enjoy this review technique. After completing a unit of material, gather together all the pictures, flash cards, and charts you have used to present the lessons. Call on various girls and boys to act as teacher for the day and let them choose one of the teaching materials. They must explain to the group how the teaching aid relates to the lesson, or tell the story connected with it. If they wish, let them use the chalkboard or a chart for their explanation. When they are

finished, they may call on others in the group to contribute any additional information they have not given, or they may ask questions of different persons in the class regarding the topic chosen. Continue this until all of the pictures, charts, or flashcards have been explained.

. The same type of approach might be used with a group instead of individual students. Assign a particular lesson to be reviewed to a group of four or five children. Let them look over the lesson and underline or write down the important points. Then give them any pictures or other teaching aids that apply to that lesson. Using the teaching aids they received, let the group present important points of the lesson through one representative or as a panel. After the presentation allow the children to ask questions of the "teacher" or panel.

The Letter Game

This is a helpful approach for reviewing names or titles of persons, places, or things, and relating them to facts the children have already learned. Prepare ahead of time a list of words that relate to one another. An example might be: baptism, children, sacrament, Jesus, Church. Write the first word on the chalkboard. Beside it, put as many dashes as there are letters in the next words on your list. Call on individuals to name letters of the alphabet, and if they belong in one of the words, let them print the letter in the correct space. If a letter does not apply, call on the next child to name one. After several letters have been filled in, ask someone to guess what the related word is. If she or he answers correctly, allow time to make a sentence out of the two related words. For example: Baptism is a sacrament; or Baptism makes us children of God; or Through baptism we share in Jesus' death and resurrection; or At baptism, we become members of the Church, the community of God's people. Continue this until all the words have been completed and put into sentences, and then have the group read them all together.

Review Mural

Tape several large pieces of newsprint to the wall or chalkboard. Assign privately to each child an important truth to be reviewed. For example: In reconciliation, Jesus forgives our sins through the priest; or, the Bible is the inspired word of God; or, God gave the ten commandments to Moses on Mt. Sinai. Invite each child to illustrate the truth with pictures, words, or diagrams on the newsprint. When all are completed, see if the group can guess what each illustration represents and to express this in a sentence. If they can't guess, call on the one who did the drawing to explain it. Add any important details they may have left out. You may also want to call on youngsters to demonstrate ways in which their illustrations are related to other illustrations in the class.

Review Sheet

Catechists are often hesitant about using simple drawings in their religion classes, but I have found that children are just as fascinated by stick figures and simple line drawings as they are by beautiful posters. Try giving each child a sheet with stick figure drawings to illustrate what they have covered in a particular lesson or unit. For example, in a third grade class, I passed out a sheet with stick figures about the story of the prodigal son. The first drawing at the bottom of the page had two stick figures, one representing the father and one the son waving good-bye with one hand and holding a bag of coins in the other. Then I drew a simple path ending in a group of box-shaped houses, some with domes. Next I drew a few stick figures to represent the boy, having fun with his friends, holding their arms in the air, and some with cups in their hands, all with smiles on their faces.

The next picture showed a fence. Behind the fence sat a stick figure representing the prodigal son, and next to him, near a puddle of water, were a few "stick pigs!" (These gave the children a laugh, which is nice to provide once in a while during your sessions.) The next picture showed a long road, with the houses in the background, and the lone figure of the prodigal walking, with a cane in his hand, back towards his own home. A stick figure of the father showed him looking out down the road for his son. And the final picture showed the father with arms outstretched, welcoming his son back. Each child received a copy of the page. Then I called on different ones to tell what they saw in each picture. We took time to discuss who had told the story and why. Then I showed a picture of a child celebrating the sacrament of reconciliation and asked how this picture was related to the story they had just been talking about. In this way, we reviewed the entire lesson we had recently covered.

Living Sentences

If you have not already used flash card definitions in your presentations, print some for the material you would like to review. The flash cards should be cut into individual words or phrases, but together should make complete sentences. For example, one sentence might read: Evangelization means/ spreading the good news/ of Jesus Christ/ and sharing our faith/ by our words and actions. (Separate the cards into words and phrases as indicated by the slashes.) Mix up all the individual cards for each definition and hand one to each child. Name one of the definitions and invite all those who have a word included in it to come to the front of the room. Ask them to line up in the proper order to form a "living sentence." Once they are lined up, ask them to read out their words and phrases in order. Then ask the group if they agree with the order of the words. If everyone agrees, have them read it together. Allow the children who are seated to ask questions about the definition and see if those holding the cards can answer their questions correctly. For example, for the above sentence they might ask: What is the good news about Jesus that we want to share? How can we share it by our words? How can we share it by our actions? Continue until all the definitions have been covered.

Flower Summary

Print several topics you have covered on large colored circles of paper. Attach these to different parts of the chalkboard, allowing space to add petals around each one. Cut out colored petals and print words on them that are related to the topics on the chalkboard. Mix up the petals and have each child choose one. Call on the children, one by one, to place their petal on the circle to which it is related. Continue this process until all the flowers are completed. Now have the group examine the petals to see if any should be changed. Ask each child to explain how his or her word is related to the circle to which it is attached. Some words may apply equally well to more than one topic. If so, be sure you make enough petals with the same phrase or word so there is one for each topic to which it relates. When all are finished, ask the youngsters to choose one of the flowers and to write or say one sentence about the topic they have chosen, using the words on the petals or others of their own choosing.

Letter Writing

Give each child a sheet of paper and ask him or her to write a letter to a friend who is not Catholic but is interested in finding out all they can about the Catholic faith. Ask them to explain to this friend what they learned about the Bible, sacraments, beatitudes, Church, Mass, or whatever topic or topics you might want to review. Offer some key words or phrases that could be included in the letter and encourage them to emphasize how their topic applies to their everyday life. When completed, ask for volunteers to share their letters with the class.

These are just a few simple ways to review material you have already covered. Don't be afraid to try new and different techniques of your own. Notice the kinds of games children play. You may be able to adapt some of them for use with your group. Each time you go over the material with them, try to help them discover new insights into it. Show your enthusiasm and enjoy the review with them. You may find that they will have a better grasp of the material and will be able to tie together in a more meaningful way the truths they have learned. Hopefully, their lives as well as their class responses will reflect this.

Summary

- Repetition is an essential element in the learning process. We do not need to make a choice between using repetition and making our lesson appealing. It is possible to accomplish the best of each of these alternatives.
- As catechists we need to change our way of perceiving repetition. We should think of it more as a reinforcement or strengthening of what the children have already learned. If we think positively of repetition, it will influence the children's attitude concerning it.
- Some helpful techniques for reinforcing what the children have learned are: Missing Lines Game, Teacher For a Day, The Letter Game, Review Mural, Review Sheet, Living Sentences, Flower Summary, and Letter Writing.
- Notice the games children play and adapt some of these to reinforce what they have learned. Helping them relate truths in a more meaningful way will influence them to do this in their own lives.

Questions for Reflection

How can I make my attitude toward repetition more positive?

Do I provide enough repetition to give the children I teach a solid grasp of what they are learning?

How can I apply the principle of repetition more effectively in my presentations?

CHAPTER 19

Learning Through Doing: A Project for Junior High

How to engage older children in a project that will help them to learn effectively

A Jesuit professor once remarked, "If you really want to learn something well, teach it!" Any catechist will agree that he or she has received from teaching as much as, if not more than, the youngsters themselves. Why not, then, give your group an opportunity to share in this kind of learning? This can be done in many ways. One that proved successful was a church tour conducted by our junior high group. It required a good bit of preparation and took time from more than one religion session, but was a great learning experience for everyone. This activity helped them learn much about their own faith and enabled them to take pride in sharing it with others.

Preparing the Group
Begin the project by taking the youngsters on a personal tour of your parish church. Emphasize the reverence we should show toward sacred places and things. Explain to them all of the following elements found in your church:

altar and tabernacle
lectern
baptismal font

crucifix
reconciliation room
sacristy
sacred vestments and vessels
statues, pictures, mosaics, stained glass windows
sanctuary lamp, candles, vigil lights
stations of the cross
choir area

The explanations need not be lengthy but should include the name of the object and its purpose. When location is significant, as for example, with altar, lectern, and baptismal font, point this out as well. Give the youngsters a chance to study each object carefully. Let them handle reverently anything they are permitted to handle, and allow them to ask questions as you go along.

In the Religion Session

If there is not sufficient time immediately after the tour, plan to devote another session to reinforcing what the teens have observed. Let them talk about what impressed them most and why. Allow them to ask any other questions that might have come to their minds. Ask each boy or girl to choose one object and to express through art or poetry what he or she learned about it, or have them write a letter to a friend who is not Catholic, explaining what they have seen and learned. Poems and letters may be posted around the room where visitors will be brought for discussion after the tour.

Challenge the youngsters to share their knowledge with others by planning a church tour for one of the younger groups. Let them make invitations to be given to the invited group. Depending on the size of your group, assign one or more of the young people to each church object or area to be explained. Ask each individual or group to write a brief explanation of the object or area as they would share it with others, recalling the explanation given by you on their initial tour. Try to keep each explanation to approximately the same length. Review the explanations with them, making corrections where necessary.

Practice Run

Before the actual event takes place, have a practice tour in church. Let each individual or group stand by his or her object or area. As you go around to each one, let them give their explanations as they would to younger children. Encourage them to speak out clearly and confidently in a conversational tone rather than recite memorized explanations.

Conducting the Tour

When the day arrives for the actual tour, give the youngsters a few minutes to get their thoughts together and to ask any last minute questions. Impress on them the fact that they should not be disturbed if they forget to mention some point. They can easily bring it up during the discussion period following the tour. Have one or two youngsters assigned to meet the visiting group as they enter the church. Begin the tour with a prayer or a hymn.

Divide the visitors into small groups of three to five children. Let one group begin as soon as you have explained where they are to start. When the first group is ready to move to the second area, wait a few moments and then send out the next group. Allow enough time between each group so that there is no overlapping. This will not be difficult if each explanation lasts approximately the same length of time. Instruct the visitors to observe and listen carefully but to save any questions they might have until after the tour. As each group finishes, have them sit in a quiet area of the church where they can reflect on what they have learned or pray quietly until the tour is completed. Or, if you prefer, guide them into the area where the junior high youngsters' posters, letters, and drawings are displayed, and allow them to examine these.

Question and Answer Period

Following the tour, a discussion should be conducted either in the quiet area of church where the visitors are already seated or in a nearby room. The junior high youngsters should sit together on one side of the room, and questions may be directed either to them or to you, but refer as many as possible to them so that they feel this is their project. When all questions have been answered, either you or your junior high teens can lead the group in a prayer of thanksgiving. Encourage them to share what they have learned with their family and their friends.

An Ecumenical Experience

This project also lends itself well to an ecumenical experience. Having explained these sacred objects to those of their own faith, the junior high group may now wish to go a step further and, as a parish activity, share their knowledge with a nearby group of another faith, or simply invite some friends who are not Catholic. If the latter is done, be sure to determine ahead of time how many persons will participate so that the sponsoring group will not be disappointed. Meet with the youngsters ahead of time to determine what changes may need to be made in their presentations. Some of the terminology may need further explanation. Ask them to imagine they are part of the visiting group and see if they can think of any questions they will need to answer. They may wish to make a small card, bookmark, or some other type of remembrance to give to each of the visitors after the tour.

Evaluating the Tour

After the tour, preferably in the following religion session, have the youngsters evaluate the project. Let them discuss what their goal was and if they think they achieved it. Let them mark on a scale how they would "grade" themselves in effort and achievement. Then ask some of the following questions:

As an individual, have I grown in knowledge of my faith through this project? If so, how?

Have we grown closer together as a faith community? In what way?

How have we shared our faith with others? How has this made me feel?

How do you think we might improve our efforts if we were to conduct this project again?

Summarize the results of the evaluation on the board for the group to see. Congratulate them on the work they did. From time to time, you may wish to refer to it again as you discuss any related material. Finally, reflect on the experience yourself and all that went into it. You may be surprised to discover that it was a learning experience for you as well as for your group.

Summary

- As a catechist, you often learn more from teaching your youngsters than they do.
- You can help them to participate in this kind of learning by having them conduct a church tour.
- To prepare your group, take them on a personal tour of your parish church, explaining to them the meaning of the important objects and places there.
- In your religion session, reinforce what they have observed through discussion. Invite each one to express through art, poetry, or a written letter what he or she has learned about some object or place in the church. Have a practice run before the actual tour is to take place.
- Before conducting the tour, allow youngsters to ask any last minute questions they may have. Divide visitors into small groups and leave enough time in between groups so there is no overlapping. Follow up the tour with a question and answer period. Allow the junior high youngsters to answer as many of the questions as possible so that they feel this is their project.
- Youngsters may wish to go a step further and conduct an ecumenical tour, inviting other nearby church groups, or friends who are not Catholic.
- After the tour is completed, preferably the following week, have the group evaluate the project. Summarize the results for them to see. Finally, reflect on the activity yourself to discover what a learning experience it was for you, as well as for your youngsters.

Questions for Reflection

Do I believe that teaching can be a rich, learning experience for me?

Do I give the youngsters in my group sufficient opportunity to grow in this way?

What activities can I plan for my group that will help to accomplish this?

CHAPTER 20

Spelling in Religion Class

*How to motivate those you teach to spell correctly
important words used in religion class*

For a long time I tried not to let it bother me. I looked at the papers the children handed in for their religion sessions and made a real effort to ignore the many misspelled words, such as "apostels," Reconsilliation," "tabrunakle," and "Eukrist." Although not all the children made mistakes like these, there were still enough examples to make it seem disrespectful to allow such distortions of religious words. However, for a long time I convinced myself that I was teaching religion, not spelling, and that there just wasn't enough time to do anything about it. Yet the nagging desire never left me. After years of "letting it be" I finally decided to do what I could to improve the situation.

Recognizing the Need
The first day I met with my religion group, I told the youngsters I would write three of their names on the chalkboard each week until I had covered the entire group. I explained that this would help me learn each one's name and that we could all get to know one another better. They seemed to like the idea. The very first day, I purposely misspelled one of the boy's names: Mikel instead of Michael. He pointed it out to me immediately, and I asked why he minded my misspelling his name. He was surprised by my question and found it difficult to give a reason. "It just isn't right," he insisted. We talked about this as a group, and I tried

to draw out from the youngsters why it might bother them to see their name misspelled. Finally, I explained that names are important because they stand for us as persons, and that we sense a certain disrespect to our person when someone is careless about spelling them. Then we talked about the many important words we would be using in religion class. "Some of these," I said, "will be taken from the Bible and others from the Church's teachings, but all of them are important because through them we come to know and relate to God better." Because of this, I explained, we owe them a certain respect. One way to show our respect is to do our best to spell them correctly. After setting the stage in this way, I tried to think of some ways in which I might reinforce the correct spelling of religious terms.

Making a Spelling List

One basic technique is to provide the group with a spelling list of religious terms that they can examine and study from time to time. When preparing your lesson plans, make a list of all the important words you want to stress. Many religion texts provide a vocabulary list with each lesson. Write these important words in a corner of the chalkboard or print them on a large card. At the beginning of your session take a few minutes to go over them with the group, pronouncing them carefully and pointing out the correct spelling. Help the children to note the words "within" words that will help them to remember the spelling more easily, for example the word "post" in apostle, "amen" in sacrament, "man" and "men" in commandment, and for the younger children, the word "us" at the end of Jesus' name.

Visualizing Words

Because visualization helps us remember, whenever you use one of these words during a lesson, show the printed card or point to the word on the chalkboard or chart and have the children take a moment to spell it. When they read from their text, have them underline these same words whenever they occur in the book.

Filling in the Blanks

During your presentation of the lesson, ask the youngsters a question such as: "What do we call the sacrament in which Jesus forgives our sins?" Instead of having the children respond in the usual way, draw as many dashes on the chalkboard as there are letters in the word. For example, if the answer is reconciliation, draw fourteen dashes in a row. Then call on individuals to guess a letter that belongs in the word. Ask the group to pay close attention as the person comes and writes this letter in the appropriate space. If someone puts a letter in the wrong place, invite someone else to come up and move the letter to the correct position. Continue until the word is finished. Then have the group say the word and spell it together.

The Spelling Tree Game

When you have completed a unit of work, play the Spelling Tree Game with your group. Look over the unit lessons before you begin teaching them. If a vocabulary list is not given, make one yourself. Include all the important words you want them to learn to spell correctly. Give copies of the list to the children or have them copy down the important words in a notebook as you teach each lesson, so that they have a complete list at the end of the unit. Ask them to go over these each week at home. When the unit is completed, go over the list carefully with them one more time.

The following week, draw an outline of a tree with branches on the chalkboard or on a large piece of posterboard. Cut out leaves of green construction paper. On the back of each leaf, write one of the words the youngsters have on their lists. Put these in a box from which they may draw. Call on one girl or boy at a time to take a leaf from the box and, without looking at the word, to hand it to you. You call out the word to be spelled. If the youngster spells it correctly, he or she attaches it to one of the tree branches with masking tape or stick tack. If the word is missed, put it back in the box so that someone else will have the chance to spell it correctly.

If your group likes competition, divide the youngsters into two teams. Draw a tree for each team and see which one can get the most leaves on their tree. Or if your group is small, put a list of the children's names on the chalkboard and give each one a star or some other symbol of recognition for a correctly spelled word.

I played the Spelling Tree Game with my group whenever I felt there was time left after completing a unit's work. What pleased me most was their eagerness. They looked forward to the end of each unit and even asked if we could take time between units to play our game. It has taken a little more effort and time to help the youngsters in this way, but I feel it has been worth it. They have a greater sense of the dignity of religious words, and a more loving respect for the God who speaks to them through these human words.

Summary

- Names are important to us and we sense a certain disrespect to our person when someone is careless about spelling them.
- Because the words that express our faith are used to help us come to know and relate better to God, we owe them a certain respect. One way to show our respect is to do our best to spell them correctly.
- Some techniques that can help reinforce correct spelling of religious words are: making a spelling list, visualizing words, filling in the blanks, and the Spelling Tree Game.
- Helping children to spell religious words correctly will help them have a more loving respect for the God who speaks to them through these human words.

Questions for Reflection

How alert am I to the mistakes my youngsters make in spelling religious words?

How important do I feel it is to correct these mistakes?

How can I, in a positive, concrete way, help the children I teach to spell religious words correctly?

CHAPTER 21

It Takes a Community

*How to involve parents and parishioners
in your faith formation program*

Do you agree with Hillary Rodham Clinton that "It takes a village" to educate a child? Whether or not you find this to be true, as a catechist you must realize that you cannot accomplish the goals of faith formation for the children you teach without the involvement of the whole community: parents and parishioners as well. Our RCIA program has done much to demonstrate this today. Years ago, when someone was interested in becoming a Catholic, he or she received private instructions from a priest. Today, inquirers learn about the faith they are to embrace in the midst of the parish. They are welcomed, taught, sponsored, sent out, blessed, and embraced by parishioners, and because of it they have a much deeper sense of what it means to belong to the community of Christ's Church.

Children are no different. It is not enough for children to come to faith formation sessions and expect that Christ "be formed" in them during the one hour to ninety minute period we may have with them. Parents, especially—whom the Church has always insisted are a child's primary educators—as well as other parishioners, must all be involved. What can we do to help this become a reality?

Using the Phone

Why not start the year off right by obtaining from your DRE the phone numbers of your children's parents? A few weeks before your sessions begin, give them a call to introduce yourself and tell the parents how pleased you are to be teaching their children this year. Give them the name of their child's textbook, what the focus of their religion lessons will be for the year, and how much you count on them to reinforce what their child will be learning. If you will be sending home parent pages, explain them briefly and encourage them to work with their child each week. Inform them of any adult religious education programs the parish may be offering.

Introducing the Year's Work

In one parish, the youth group volunteered to work with the children in the elementary grades for their opening session, while each catechist met with the parents of the children in her or his group. For one hour, each catechist presented to the parents what their goals were for the year, and went through the children's textbook with them, showing what would be emphasized during the coming year, pointing out the pages reserved especially for use at home, the prayers and Catholic rituals and practices that would be covered that year, and other ways in which the parents might work with their children at home. Parents learned how the material was presented to their children and how important their support was. Many stayed afterwards to thank the catechists for the insights they had received, and parental cooperation was much more evident that year.

Adult Religious Formation Sessions

Another suggestion would be to invite the parents to attend adult religious formation sessions while their children are meeting with their groups. In one parish where this was done, the DRE gave an adult presentation of the major themes covered in the faith formation program, and the parents could ask any questions they might have about their child's sessions. Needless to say, having their parents learning along with them will impress the children with the importance of their own religious formation.

Inviting Parents to Religion Sessions

Many catechists invite parents to attend some of the children's sessions. This gives parents a first-hand view of how you are the messenger, letting God form Christ in their children, and how the children are grasping the basics of their Catholic faith. One fourth grade catechist invited the parents of her children to come and participate in a brief review of the material she had covered in one unit. The parents showed a new interest when they discovered more about what their children were learning and the new ways in which it was being presented to them. Many also admitted that it made them realize their own need to grow in their faith. In another parish, catechists set up times to meet with parents to discuss their child's progress after each unit's work was completed.

Parental Interviews and Witnesses

In a very large southern parish, the DRE scheduled interviews with parents of children who were about to celebrate the sacraments of reconciliation and Eucharist, and confirmation. Interviews were conducted in an informal way by the pastor, the DRE, and other qualified parishioners. In this way, both parents and other parishioners were involved in the children's preparation. The interviews covered questions that focused on Christian formation in the home such as:

1. Why do you want your child to receive First Holy Communion?
2. Are you bringing your child to Sunday Mass? Are you able to assist your child in understanding the Mass?
3. Does your child take part in the special Liturgy of the Word for children? How has that helped him or her?
4. Are you able to discuss the readings or homily with your child?
5. What things do you do at home to make your faith more visible, more alive for your child? Do you pray together? Do you have religious books or symbols in your home?
6. How do you and your children talk over moral questions?
7. What are some things you do to help your child develop a stronger faith in and love for Jesus? A stronger sense of Christian conscience?
8. How can your parish help your family more?
9. Do you have any questions about the parish's religious education program, or suggestions for improving it?

In this parish, children who celebrated the Mass preceding the religious education program on Sunday took part in a special Liturgy of the Word during the Mass. Inviting parents or other parishioners to take turns leading them in this activity is another way of involving them in the religious formation of their children.

In this same parish, the children celebrated special prayer services in preparation for the sacraments. At these services, parents were called on to give witness to their faith and their love for the Eucharist.

Family Banners

Another project that has become quite common in many parishes is having those in the sacramental preparation program work with their families to make banners expressing their thoughts and feelings about celebrating the sacrament. In this way, parents and children are able to share their faith lives in an exciting and personal way. The banners are then hung in an appropriate place in the parish church on the day the sacrament is celebrated, so that the entire parish may join in the celebration. Some parishes hang them in the front of the church, while others place them on the pews where the families will be sitting.

Prayer Sponsors

In another parish, parishioners were invited to select from a chart the name of a child preparing to receive the sacraments, and to sponsor that child by praying for him or her during their time of preparation. Older, housebound parishioners, especially, welcomed this opportunity as a way for them to participate in the parish church's ministry, and some formed special ties with the child long after they had celebrated the sacraments.

Parish Dramatizations and Programs

Everyone, and most especially parents, love to see their children perform. Many parishes invite parents and others to work with the children to perform a Christmas play or a musical program. Why not think about sponsoring a program where the children share what they are learning about in their religion classes? For example, first graders might present something about creation, second graders something about the Eucharist, third graders something about the Church, and so on, choosing whichever theme is covered in their sessions for that year. Parents and other interested parishioners can be very inventive in helping to plan and organize these programs.

Inviting Speakers

Another way of involving parents and other parishioners in the religious formation of your children is to invite them to be speakers at your sessions. Inviting a priest, a sister, or a deacon to speak to the children when you are teaching about vocations is always most effective. In one parish, a couple was invited to speak to a fifth grade group during their lesson on the sacrament of Christian marriage. When teaching the children about the works of mercy, why not invite a member of the St. Vincent de Paul society to tell the children about their work? For your lesson on baptism, you may want to invite a newly baptized adult to share with the children his or her experience of the catechumenate. There are many opportunities for you to involve members of the parish community. Be sure to give each guest a specific idea about what you are teaching so that they can coordinate their presentation with it, plus a time frame in which to present it.

Of course, there will always be some parents who will not be able to take part in these opportunities. Keep in touch with them by either phoning them or sending home short notes about their child's participation and progress. Try to be as positive as possible, but if there is a problem with a child's participation, ask for the parent's suggestions and cooperation. You will find that few parents do not wish the best for their children.

Whatever your circumstances, do your best to involve parents and parishioners in your formation program in whatever way possible. It will help you realize that you do not face this ministry of Christian initiation alone. And it will give both parents and parishioners a greater sense of awareness that they all contribute to the Christian initiation of their children, and to the building up of their faith community.

Summary

- One hour (or ninety minutes) a week is not enough for the religious formation of our children. Parents, as well as other parishioners, must be involved.
- Some ways of involving both parents and parishioners in the religious formation of your children are: phone calls to parents, introducing the year's work, adult religious formation sessions, inviting parents to

attend religion sessions, parental interviews and witnesses, involving parents and parishioners in the Liturgy of the Word for children, making family banners, prayer sponsors, parish dramatization programs, and inviting speakers to your religion sessions.

- Contact parents who are not able to take part in any of these activities by phoning them or sending home short notes about their child's participation and progress. Meet with them, especially at the beginning of the year.
- Involving parents and other parishioners in this way will help you realize that you are not working alone, and will also give both parents and parishioners a greater sense of awareness that they all, as a community, contribute to the Christian initiation of their children.

Questions for Reflection

Am I convinced of the importance of involving the whole community—parents and parishioners—in the task of faith formation?

How do I involve parents and other parishioners in the faith formation of these children? What more can I do?

Is There a Place For Fun?

How to use games and puzzles to demonstrate
that learning the faith can be fun

Some people have the mistaken notion that religious learning excludes fun, for the catechist as well as for the children. Yet nothing is further from the truth. Recently on the Internet there was a series of pictures showing a smiling Jesus surrounded by children. The Jesus we know and love has a special place in his heart for children and during his earthly lifetime must have joined in their laughter and enjoyed their play. As a young boy, Jesus must have played children's games with his friends and neighbors. And we know from Lk 7:32 that, as an adult, he also observed children at play. As catechists, we know from our own observation that playing games and working puzzles make up a very large part of a child's experience. Why not utilize them, then, as already popular instruments for learning in a fun-filled way? In many of the previous chapters there are suggestions for fun ways to make your religion sessions more interesting. Here are a few other possibilities that may encourage you to plan some of your own.

PRIMARY GRADES

Spin the Wheel

This is a simple game you can use with young children to review topics such as God, creation, Jesus, and so forth, using pictures and questions from that material.

Materials needed: Large piece of poster board, one large brad fastener, tape, pictures used in previous lessons (preferably small ones), and slips of paper with questions about what the children have already learned.

Directions: Cut a large circle (approximately 24 inches in diameter) and a simple spinner out of posterboard. Cut a small hole in the center of the spinner and attach it to the center of the circle with the brad, loosely enough so that it can spin around.

Divide the wheel into sections (six or eight, depending on the size of the pictures you will insert). Assign one section to each topic. In each section, attach with tape as many small pictures as will fit that pertain to the topic you wish to review.

On small slips of paper, write questions covering these topics. Fold the slips of paper and put a question mark on the outside of each. Tape these around the pictures in the section to which they pertain.

Ask the children to take turns spinning the wheel. Invite each one to choose a question or a picture in the section where the arrow stops. If a child chooses a question, ask him or her to read it aloud and answer it. If a picture is chosen, ask the child to hold up the picture and explain what she or he remembers learning about it.

Award a sticker or a star to each child who answers a question or explains a picture satisfactorily.

All About Jesus Puzzle
This is a simple puzzle about the life of Jesus that can be used in the lower grades. For very young children, you may want to draw the crossword grid on the chalkboard or on a large sheet of posterboard. Read the clues out to the children, and call on volunteers to respond. If the children are able to write out their answers, have them say the correct answer and then write it in the grid. If they are not able to write it, have them say the correct word, and then you print the answer for them and have the group read it together.

INTERMEDIATE GRADES

Sacrament Search

This game may be used to review what your group has learned during the year about the sacraments. It can be adapted for the commandments, beatitudes, corporal or spiritual works of mercy, and so forth.

Materials needed: Two large sheets of newsprint, two different colored markers, seven envelopes (one for each sacrament,) with at least eight questions about that sacrament on folded slips of paper in each envelope.

Directions: With a black marker draw the outline of a large, wide S on the newsprint. Do the same on a second sheet of newsprint. On each chart, divide the outline of the S into 28 horizontal spaces, each wide enough to place an X in each space. At every fourth space write the name of one of the sacraments, beginning with baptism, then Eucharist, and ending with holy orders.

Divide your group into two teams and choose a leader for each team. Assign a chart to each team. Give each leader one of the colored markers so that he or she can mark the chart with the team's color whenever they answer correctly. Draw ballots to see which team goes first.

The leader of the first team draws a question from the envelope for baptism and asks it. Anyone from that team may answer the question after being called on by the leader. If the answer is correct, the leader marks an X with his or her team's marker in the first space on their chart, moving toward baptism. If the question is not answered correctly, the question is returned to the envelope. If there is uncertainty about the response, the catechist should judge its correctness.

The leader of the second team then takes a turn at drawing a question and follows the same procedure. If answered correctly, the leader places an X with his team's color in the first space on their chart. Continue taking turns. When a team has reached the baptism space, they answer the fourth question about that sacrament. Then, on its next turn, the team begins to answer questions from the Eucharist envelope. Continue this procedure with each team until one of them has reached the holy orders space. The first team to arrive there wins the game.

Living for Jesus Puzzle

This puzzle for the middle grades reviews some of the things that Jesus asks us to do as his followers. You may wish to draw the grid on the chalkboard, or on posterboard and give the youngsters a sheet listing the clues. Let them look over the clues and then call on them one by one to fill in any which they think they can answer correctly. Or you may want to have copies of the empty grid, with the clues at the bottom, have them work on these at their desks, and then go over the answers with them.

UPPER GRADES

Tic Tac Go

This game for older youngsters can be used to review their knowledge of important persons, places, and events they have learned about in previous lessons.

Materials needed: Chalkboard, chalk, slips of paper, pen or pencil, masking tape.

Directions: Divide the group into two teams, one for X and one for O. On the chalkboard, draw a very large square and divide it into nine equal sections.

On slips of paper, write out questions about persons, places, or events that you have covered in previous lessons. Fold the slips of paper in half. For those pertaining to persons, write a large PE on the front, for those about places, write PL, and those about events, EV. Attach one of each type of question to each of the nine sections on the chalkboard.

Have the persons on each team draw numbers to see in what order they will take their turns.

The person to go first chooses one of the slips of paper from any section he or she would like. If this person answers the question on the slip of paper correctly, his or her team's mark (X or O) is placed in the square. If the question is not answered, or cannot be answered correctly (the catechist is the judge of this), it is attached back to the same square from which it was taken.

Next, a person from the opposite team chooses a slip of paper. It may be taken from any space unmarked with a team's X or O, and includes any unanswered or incorrectly answered question. If the second player's question is answered correctly, he or she puts the team mark in that square. Once a team's letter is placed in a square, no other question can be taken from that square until the next round.

Continue this procedure until one or the other team has three of their marks in a row, going in any direction.

Once the first team has won, continue playing two more rounds, until all the questions have been answered. The team to win the most rounds is declared Top Winner.

The Ministry of Jesus Puzzle

This puzzle for the upper grades is based on some of the miracles and parables of Jesus. You may wish to make copies of the blank grid with the clues, give these to the youngsters to work on at their desks and then go over the answers with them. If you wish, you may have them look up the answers in their Bibles. Or, as a variation, you may want to give them a grid with the answers, then give the clues but not in order, and have them find the correct answers on their grid. Another suggestion might be to have them look over the grid with the answers, and ask them to write clues for each one. (See puzzle at end of Appendix.)

All about Jesus

ACROSS

1. The town where Jesus was born.
5. Jesus came to bring_____to the world.
6. Talking with God is called _____.
9. Jesus died on the _____to save us.
11. Jesus' apostles asked him to teach them to _____.
12. The mother of Jesus.
15. We celebrate Jesus' rising from the dead on _____ Sunday.
18. Jesus asks us to love each _____.
19. Jesus said, "_____the little children come to me."
20. Jesus said that whatever we _____for in his name, the Father will give us.
21. On Christmas night angels sang "Glory to God in high heaven, and peace on _____."

DOWN
1. The sacrament which makes us children of God.
2. One reason we pray is to _____ God for all the blessings we have received.
3. Jesus came to save _____.
4. What Jesus wants us to say to sin.
5. The foster father of Jesus, and husband of Mary.
7. At the Last Supper, Jesus told the apostles to take and _____ his body.
8. Jesus showed by his example how we should _____ our parents.
10. The Son of God and our Savior.
13. Jesus remained on earth forty days _____ his resurrection.
14. What Jesus always said to his Father's will.
16. On Easter Sunday, Jesus _____ from the dead.
17. Jesus taught us to always do our _____ in all things.

ANSWERS

ACROSS
1. Bethlehem
5. joy
6. prayer
9. cross
11. pray
12. Mary
15. Easter
18. other
19. let
20. ask
21. earth

DOWN
1. Baptism
2. thank
3. everyone
4. no
5. Joseph
7. eat
8. obey
10. Jesus
13. after
14. yes
16. rose
17. best

Living for Jesus

ACROSS

1. If we respect what belongs to others, we will always be _____.
4. The third commandment tells us to honor God's _____.
6. Those who live for Jesus keep away from _____.
7. True followers of Jesus never hurt their friends _____ their enemies.
8. If we live for _____ in this life, we will share his happiness forever.
9. Jesus said, "_____ you love me, keep my commandments."
13. Jesus asks us to love, respect, and _____ our parents.
15. A follower of Jesus _____ what he has with those in need.
16. We must love others _____ we cannot be followers of Jesus.
17. To love God and to love others are the two _____ commandments.
19. Living for Jesus means always trying to say _____ to God in all things.
21. If we love others as Jesus did, we will always try not to _____ them.

23. If we are faithful followers of Jesus, we will share his happiness in _____someday.
25. When we are truly _____for our sins, we try to do better.
27. Jesus taught us to love all persons, no matter what color their _____is.
28. Jesus said that he who _____his Father's will is his true follower.

DOWN

1. Jesus said that what we do to others, we do to _____.
2. We celebrate Jesus' birth _____Christmas day.
3. Those who live for Jesus always speak the _____.
4. Each day we offer to God all that we think, _____, or say.
5. Jesus said that we _____his followers if we have love for one another.
8. The gift that comes to those who live for Jesus is _____.
10. What Jesus asks us to do when others have hurt us.
11. What we should do when we are tempted to sin.
12. Jesus told us that anyone who _____a favor of God in his name will receive it.
14. Jesus said we must love _____those who hate us.
18. We pray to ask God's blessings and to _____God for his many gifts.
20. If we are faithful to Jesus, we will live with him for _____.
22. Jesus showed us that good is stronger than evil when he _____from the dead.
24. Jesus said, "_____ and you shall receive."
26. What Jesus always said to his Father's will.

ANSWERS

ACROSS		**DOWN**	
1. honest	16. or	1. him	12. asks
4. day	17. great	2. on	14. even
6. sin	19. yes	3. truth	18. thank
7. or	21. hurt	4. do	20. ever
8. Jesus	23. heaven	5. are	22. rose
9. if	25. sorry	8. joy	24. ask
13. obey	27. skin	10. forgive	26. yes
15. shares	28. does	11. pray	

Ministry of Jesus

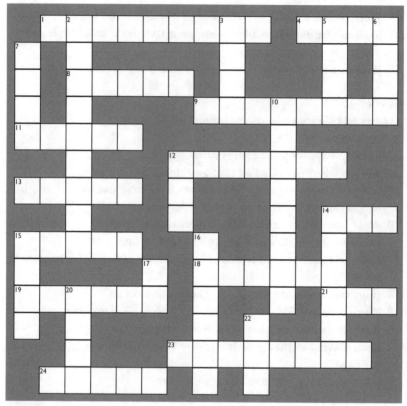

ACROSS

1. Jesus cured this man's servant because of his great faith (Mt 8:5)
4. At the Last Supper, Jesus said to Thomas, "If you really knew me, you would _____ my Father also." (Jn 14:7)
8. Jesus said to be his followers we must take up our _____each day. (Lk 9:23)
9. Jesus said, "I am the Good _____." (Jn 10:14)
11. In the parable of the Rich Man and Lazarus, the rich man was punished because he refused to _____his gifts. (Lk 16:19–31)
12. On Holy Thursday, Jesus sent Peter and John to_____the Passover meal. (Lk 22:8)
13. Jesus cured the blind Bartimeus because of his _____ . (Mk 10:52)
14. Jesus said that he came, not to abolish the _____ but to fulfill it. (Mt 5:17)
15. The enemy of God's kingdom is called _____.

18. After his arrest, Annas the high _____ and Caiphas questioned Jesus. (Jn 1:19–24)
19. In the sacrifice of the cross, Jesus was both _____and high priest.
21. Jesus said, "No servant can serve _____masters." (Lk 16:13)
23. Jesus' _____was one of service to others.
24. Jesus always showed _____to sinners. (Lk 15:2)

DOWN

2. At the Last Supper, Jesus gave us himself in the bread of the _____. (Lk 22:17)
3. At Jesus' trial, many false witnesses spoke against Jesus under _____. (Mk 14:56)
5. Jesus told us that he came in his Father's _____. (Jn 5:43)
6. Jesus came to proclaim to us the _____of God.
7. At the Last Supper, Jesus promised that whoever _____anything of the Father in his name, will receive it. (Jn 16:23)
10. Jesus told a parable about a tax collector and a _____who went to the temple to pray. (Lk 18:10)
12. Jesus told us that when we _____our hand to the plow, we must not look back again. (Lk 9:62)
14. Some of the religious leaders in Jesus' time were more concerned with the _____ of the Law than with the spirit.
15. When a storm came up at sea, the apostles came to Jesus and said "Lord, _____us!" (Mt 8:25)
16. Jesus promised to send the Holy _____to guide us. (Jn 14:16)
17. Jesus said, "I _____ the bread of life." (Jn 6:35)
20. Jesus said "No one can _____to me unless the Father who sent me draws him" (Jn 6:44)
22. The Father sent Jesus into the world that those who believe in him might never _____. (Jn 3:16)

ANSWERS

Across		Down	
1. centurion	14. law	2. Eucharist	14. letter
4. know	15. Satan	3. oath	15. save
8. cross	18. priest	5. name	16. spirit
9. shepherd	19. victim	6. word	17. am
11. share	21. two	7. asks	20. come
12. prepare	23. ministry	10. Pharisee	22. die
13. faith	24. mercy	12. put	

Using Dramatization

*How to involve your whole class
in a Christmas and an Easter play.*

I have always been delighted with the eagerness children show for
dramatization. They seem to have a natural instinct for it. You may
remember times in your own childhood when you enjoyed acting out
different roles or situations. Dramatization of Scripture stories can be
real learning experiences for the children in your class. It is important
to keep these short and simple when using them as part of a lesson. But
for the great liturgical seasons of Christmas and Easter, many catechists
plan more elaborate dramatizations, and often parents are invited to
these. Here are two plays, one for the Christmas season and another for
Eastertime, which can involve every child in your class in some way.
Some might be actors and others part of a chorus that recites and inter-
prets prayers or songs; still others may be singers in the choir.

THE CHRISTMAS STORY

Participants:

Narrator, Mary, Joseph, Infant, Shepherds, Angels, Singers, Reciters

Scenes:

1) The appearance of the angels to the shepherds
2) The birth of Jesus at Bethlehem
3) The gathering around the crib

(The acting scenes would be best performed in the center of the room
with the reciters and singers on either side)

Props:

On one side of the room, a simple stable or cave may be constructed out
of large cardboard boxes, with a small wooden or cardboard box filled

with straw as a manger. On the opposite side, the shepherd's field might be set up with green outdoor/indoor carpeting and rocks made from large, crumpled up brown bags. All of the characters should be dressed simply with robes made of sheets, scarves, bathrobes, or pieces of fabric.

SCENE 1 The appearance of the angels to the shepherds.

Singers	(Hum the music to "It Came Upon a Midnight Clear.")
Reciters	(Recite together slowly and reverently the words of the hymn, emphasizing the italicized words and accompanying their recitation with simple gestures described here.)
	It came upon a *midnight* clear (extend hands upward)
	That *glorious* song of old (move hands down in circular fashion)
	From *angels* bending *near the earth* (slowly bow head and fold hands)
	To *touch* their *harps of gold* (bring hands together as if playing strings of harp)
	Peace on the earth (extend hands forward and then in circle as shape of world)
	Good will to *men* (move hands forward in a giving gesture)
	From *heaven's* all *gracious* king (hands raised upward in adoration)
	The *world* in *solemn stillness* lay (bring hands slowly down toward sides)
	To *hear* the *angels* sing (arms up, ending with folded hands and faces looking up)
Actors	(A group of shepherds is seated around as if tending their sheep. Some have their heads down as if sleeping, others are seated around an imaginary fire, rubbing their hands together to keep them warm. An angel appears on

	the scene as mentioned in the following reading.)
Narrator	(Reads Luke 2:8–10 slowly and reverently.) There were shepherds in that locality, living in the fields, and keeping night watch by turns over their flocks. The angel of the Lord appeared to them as the glory of the Lord shone around them and they were very much afraid. The angel said to them:
Angel	You have nothing to fear! I come to proclaim good news to you—tidings of great joy to be shared by the whole people. This day in David's city, a savior has been born to you, the messiah and the lord. Let this be a sign to you: In a manger you will find an infant wrapped in swaddling clothes.
Narrator	Suddenly, there was with the angel, a multitude of the heavenly host praising God and saying
Singers	(Sing joyfully the chorus from "Angels We Have Heard on High") Gloria in excelsis Deo. Gloria in excelsis Deo.
Narrator	(Continues reading Luke 2:15) When the angels had returned to heaven, the shepherds said to one another
Shepherds	Let us go over to Bethlehem and see this event which the Lord has made known to us. (Shepherds exit slowly)
Singers	(Hum quietly "Angels We Have Heard on High" as shepherds exit.)

Intermission

Scene 2 The Birth of Jesus at Bethlehem

Actors (Mary is kneeling by a manger, looking down at the infant Jesus. Joseph stands by her side, as if protecting them both.)

Singers (Hum softly the melody of "What Child is This?")

Reciters (While singers are humming, the reciters speak the words of the song and interpret the words with bodily motions.) What child is this (point both arms down, with palms raised, toward infant)
Who laid to rest
On Mary's lap is sleeping (overlap arms as if cradling infant)
Whom angels greet with anthems sweet (extend arms outward shoulder length, as if in prayer)
While shepherds, watch are keeping. (right hands over eyes, looking outward)
This, this is Christ the King (extend hands toward infant)
Whom shepherds guard and angels sing (extend hands forward with palms facing down as if in blessing)
This, this is Christ the King (bring hands together and bow heads)
The Babe, the son of Mary. (extend hands towards Mary and infant)

Narrator (Reads Luke 2:16)
So the shepherds went in haste and found Mary and Joseph, and the infant lying in the manger.

Actors (The shepherds walk in quietly as the narrator begins. Some stand and bow their heads reverently, others kneel around the manger. Mary looks up and smiles at them, extending her hand toward the infant or holding the infant up for them to see.)

Singers   (Softly hum the first verse of "Silent Night")

Reciters   (Slowly recite the words to the first verse of "Silent
                      Night" while the singers hum.)
                      Silent night, holy night
                      All is calm, all is bright
                      Round yon virgin, mother and child
                      Holy infant so tender and mild
                      Sleep in heavenly peace,
                      Sleep in heavenly peace.

Singers   (Sing the melody and words to the second verse of
                      "Silent Night")
                      Silent night, holy night
                      Shepherds quake at the sight
                      Glories stream from heaven afar
                      Heavenly hosts sing alleluia
                      Christ the Savior is born
                      Christ the Savior is born.

SCENE 3: Gathering Around the Crib

Narrator   Christmas did not just happen yesterday. Jesus comes
                      and is present among us every day. Like the shepherds,
                      we only need our faith to recognize him. He comes in
                      those who need love, hope, comfort, and joy in their
                      lives. He comes in those who bring these same gifts to
                      others. He comes in every circumstance of our lives.
                      Mary invites us to come and adore Jesus as the shep-
                      herds did that first Christmas night.

Singers   (Begin humming "O Come All Ye Faithful" as far as the
                      words, "joyful and triumphant." Then stop a moment
                      and begin again.)

Reciters   (Begin reciting the words when the singers start humming the song a second time, and accompany the words with gestures.)

O come, all ye faithful (extend arms toward audience, in invitation)

Joyful and triumphant (raise hands outward and upward to express joy)

O come ye, o come ye, to Bethlehem (extend hands toward crib in invitation)

Come and behold him (extend both arms reverently toward infant)

Born the king of angels (extend arms outward in winglike motion)

O come, let us adore him (fold hands and bow heads)

O come, let us adore him (bow heads and upper body lower)

O come, let us adore him (begin opening hands and arms outward)

Christ the Lord. (continue bringing hands farther and farther outward until the song is ended.)

Singers   (Sing the second verse of "O Come all Ye Faithful," and invite the audience to gather around the crib and join in the singing.)

Sing, choirs of angels

Sing in exaltation

Sing all ye citizens of heaven above.

Glory to God, in the highest.

O come, let us adore him.

O come, let us adore him.

O come, let us adore him,

Christ the Lord.

(At the end of the Christmas play, invite all those present to join in singing some favorite Christmas hymns.)

And What About Easter?

Although the resurrection of Jesus is the central mystery of our faith, and Easter the greatest feast in the Church year, we so seldom celebrate this feast with our students. Perhaps it is because Holy Week, taken up with teachings on the Eucharist and Christ's passion, is customarily followed by Easter vacation. There is always opportunity, however, for celebrating Christ's resurrection during the weeks following Easter. Our students need to be reminded that the Church does not abruptly end her celebration on Easter Sunday just because the rest of society does. Indeed, because of the importance of this feast, the Church extends the Easter season for several weeks. This is an appropriate time to celebrate the resurrection in our classrooms. The following dramatization, based entirely on John's gospel account, might be presented by an individual class or by a group of small classes. It includes enough parts for all your children to participate.

AN EASTER PLAY

Participants:
Narrator, Chorus, Jesus, Mary Magdalene, Two Angels, Eleven Apostles (Judas is missing from the group, and Thomas is not present for Jesus' first appearance.)

Scenes:
1) A Visit to the Tomb
2) Jesus Appears to the Apostles

Props:
Props should be kept as simple as possible. Allow the children to help prepare them ahead of time if possible. A large room is needed, divided into two sections. One corner may serve as the upper room in Jerusalem where the apostles meet. You may want to have a few small rugs or towels scattered around on the floor for them to sit on, or a low table at which they may be seated.

In another corner, at a distance, a cave may be constructed of large brown crumpled paper bags taped together and to the wall. Some cardboard boxes may be hidden inside to support the cave, and two stools beneath the "tomb" where the angels might sit. There should be a large opening at the cave front, through which can be seen the tomb, made out of two or three sturdy boxes, painted or covered with grey or light brown paper. At one end of the tomb, place a white sheet crumpled and hanging down to the floor. At the other end, a smaller white cloth wrapped around like a head covering should be neatly laid out.

The students may wish to wear simple robes, made of small sheets draped over the shoulders or bathrobes. Jesus should be dressed in white, with some gold trim if desired. Angels should also be dressed in white.

SCENE 1	**A Visit to the Tomb** (The apostles enter slowly, with bowed heads, and seat themselves around the room.)
Narrator	The apostles gathered quietly and sadly in the upper room in Jerusalem where they had celebrated the Last Supper with Jesus. Jesus had died and was buried. He had been everything to them, and now he was gone. Their hope was buried with him. They tried to stay close together for support, but their hearts were heavy. (Have the chorus, standing near the cave begin humming slowly and softly the three Alleluias from the Easter liturgy.)
Narrator	Early in the morning on the first day of the week, while it was still dark, Mary Magdalene came to the tomb. (Mary Magdalene walks slowly toward the cave and peers inside.)
Narrator	Mary saw that the stone had been moved away, so she ran off to Simon Peter and the other disciple John. (Mary runs toward upper room)
Mary Magdalene	The Lord has been taken from the tomb! We don't know where they have put him! (Peter and John leave the room hurriedly, while the

other apostles begin talking excitedly to one another. John arrives at the tomb before Peter. Mary follows behind at some distance.)

Narrator   At that, Peter and John started toward the tomb. They were running side by side, but John reached the tomb first. He did not enter, but bent down to peer in, and saw the wrappings lying on the ground.
(John peers inside the cave.)

Narrator   Presently, Simon Peter came along behind him and entered the tomb. (Peter goes to entrance of cave and steps in.)
He observed the wrappings on the ground and saw the piece of cloth which had covered the head rolled up in a place by itself. Then John went in.
(John moves up close to Peter.)
He saw and believed. Remember, as yet they did not understand the Scripture that Jesus had to rise from the dead. With this the disciples returned home.
(Peter and John walk slowly back to the upper room, lost in thought. Mary remains behind, and walks up close to the tomb. She buries her head in her hands as if weeping.)

Narrator   Meanwhile, Mary stood weeping beside the tomb. Even as she wept, she stopped to peer inside, and there she saw two angels in dazzling robes.
(Two angels appear in the cave as Mary peers inside. Have them "sit" on the ends of the tomb, if possible.)

Narrator   One was seated at the head and the other at the foot of the place where Jesus had lain.

Angel   Woman, why are you weeping?
Mary   Because the Lord has been taken away and I do not

know where they have laid him.

Narrator	She had no sooner said this, than she turned around and caught sight of Jesus standing there. (Jesus comes forward.) But she did not know him.
Jesus	Woman, why are you weeping? Who is it that you are looking for? (Mary stands, with head bowed low, and then slowly, looks up.)
Narrator	She supposed he was the gardener, so she said....
Mary	Sir, if you are the one who carried him off, tell me where you have laid him and I will take him away.
Jesus	(Extends his arms toward Mary and says with great love....) Mary!
Mary	(Looks up surprised and overjoyed, then falls to her knees and reaches out toward Jesus as she says:) Rabbi! Teacher!
Jesus	Do not cling to me, for I have not yet ascended to the Father. Rather, go to my followers and tell them, "I am ascending to my Father and your Father, to my God and your God."
Narrator	Mary Magdalene went to the disciples.
Mary	(Mary gets up and walks quickly in the direction of the upper room, and says to the apostles:) I have seen the Lord!
Narrator	Then she reported what he had said to her.

Chorus	(Chorus comes forward and recites or sings the first verse of an appropriate Easter hymn.)

INTERMISSION

SCENE 2:	**Jesus Appears to the Apostles** (Ten apostles are seated in groups in the upper room, talking together. Thomas is absent. There is a sudden excitement in the air.)
Narrator	On the evening of the first day of the week, even though the disciples had locked the doors of the place where they were for fear of the Jews, Jesus came and stood before them.
Jesus	(Enters the room, with arms extended toward the apostles.) Peace be with you. (The apostles look up in surprise.)
Narrator	(Jesus holds out his hands and points to his side where the spear entered his body.) When he had said this, he showed them his hands and his side. At the sight of the Lord, the apostles rejoiced.
Jesus	Peace be with you. As the Father has sent me, so I send you.
Narrator	Then he breathed on them and said....
Jesus	(Extends his hands over apostles in blessing) If you forgive sins, they are forgiven them; if you hold them bound, they are held bound. (As the apostles are grouped around Jesus, some standing, some kneeling with heads bowed, Jesus slips out quietly. After a few moments, the apostles stand together, waving their arms in wonderment and talking excitedly. Then Thomas walks in.)

Narrator	It happened that one of the twelve, Thomas, was absent when Jesus came. The other disciples kept telling him:
Apostles	(With great excitement) We have seen the Lord!
Thomas	(Looks at the apostles with disbelief.) I will never believe it without touching the nail prints in his hands, without putting my finger in the nail marks on his feet, and my hand into his side. (All of the apostles shake their heads in disbelief and disappointment at Thomas' response. Then, they go off by themselves. Some sit with their heads buried in their laps, on the floor, as if asleep. Others may sit at the table and lay their heads down.)
Chorus	(Recites or sings the second verse of the Easter hymn.)
Narrator	A week later, the disciples were once more in the room, and this time Thomas was with them. (Apostles lift their heads. Some get up and walk around. Others begin to talk quietly among themselves. Thomas is with them.)
Narrator	Despite the locked doors, Jesus came and stood before them.
Jesus	Peace be with you. (Turns to Thomas who drops to his knees in awe) Take your finger and examine my hands. Put your hand into my side. Do not persist in your unbelief, but believe.
Thomas	(The apostle reaches up toward Jesus, then bows his head and says with great reverence) My Lord and my God!

Jesus   You became a believer because you saw me. Blest are they who have not seen and have believed.
                   (Jesus remains in the center of the room, with hands extended over Thomas and the other apostles.)

Narrator   And so, the risen Jesus remains with us today—with us, his followers, who have not seen and yet believe. We rejoice with the Lord in his victory over sin and death, and work each day to witness to his love and forgiveness.

Chorus   (Chorus sings the third verse of the Easter hymn.)

At the end of the play, invite all those present to join with the chorus in singing some Easter Alleluias or another joyful Easter hymn.

Resources for the Great Catechist

Klein, Rev. Peter, editor. *Catholic Source Book*
   Brown & ROA, Dubuque, IA, 1990. An invaluable resource book for
   Catholics, containing prayers and information in all areas of the
   Catholic faith, Scripture, liturgy, the saints, symbols, and word and
   phrase origins.

_____. Liguori Kids Heroes Series.
   Liguori Publications, One Liguori Drive, Liguori, MO
   These pamphlets introduce kids to modern day heroes who have
   changed the world for the better by their faith, their courage, and by
   their willingness to do the right thing.

McCarty, Jim. *The Confident Catechist*
   Brown & ROA, Dubuque, IA
   A collection of practical, helpful tips on motivation, use of audiovi-
   suals, parental involvement, and avoiding burnout.

Mueller Nelson, Gertrude. *A Walk Through Our Church*
   Paulist Press, NY/Mahwah, NJ
   A simply presented and reverent guided tour through church for
   children, with names and explanations of church articles and fur-
   nishings.

O'Keefe, Susan & H.M. Alan. *What Does a Nun Do? What Does a Priest Do?*
   Paulist Press, NY, Mahwah, NJ
   A charming two-in-one book that humanizes priests and sisters,
   showing that they laugh, cry, work, play, and pray in a very human,
   friendly, and approachable way.

Petro, Valerie L. & Lauren E. Marley. *Family Friendly Web Sites (for Kids)*
   Paulist Press, NY/Mahwah, NJ
   A guide to safe, educational, and fun web sites for Christian parents
   and their children.

Pinto, Matthew & Kathleen Andes. *Friendly Defenders*
   Ascension Press, P.O. Box 1990, West Chester, PA
   Attractive Catholic flash cards, covering fifty of the most commonly
   asked questions people have about the Catholic faith, with easy to
   understand answers. For use at home, in religion classes, or at
   church.

Shanley, Jim & Betsy. *Holy Traders Cards*
   Azariah Company, Boynton Beach, FL
   A series of forty cards on the saints, with dates of birth and death,
   an overview of their accomplishments, canonization information,
   and a prayer to each saint, along with other helpful information
   such as the spiritual and corporal works of mercy, the beatitudes,
   grace, conversion, and religious objects.

Stanton, Sue. *Child's Guide to the Mass*
   Paulist Press, NY/Mahwah, NJ
   In a fun and engaging way, this book guides children through the
   main parts of the Mass so they can understand and appreciate what
   is going on.

Wallace, Susan Helen, fsp. *Saints for Young Readers for Every Day*
   Pauline Books & Media, 50 St. Paul's Avenue, Boston, MA
   These short biographies of the saints focus on the example they give
   to children of the Christian virtues.

Berger, Alison. *I Like Being in Parish Ministry: Catechist.*
   Twenty Third Publications, P.O. Box 180, Mystic, CT
   With stories, reflection questions, and concrete suggestions, invites
   catechists to probe the heart of their vocation: to help those they
   minister with to know, celebrate, live, and contemplate the mystery
   of Christ.

Costello, Gwen. *A Prayerbook for Catechists.*
   Twenty Third Publications, Mystic, CT
   Offer prayers from the heart for a variety of seasons and situations.

Glavich, Mary Kathleen, SND. *Acting Out the Miracles and Parables*
Twenty Third Publications, Mystic, CT
Fifty two playlets for grades one through six that will enliven and
enrich religion classes.

Glavich, Mary Kathleen, SND. *Leading Students Into Scripture*
Twenty Third Publications, Mystic, CT
A wide range of methods for helping children understand and
appreciate the Bible.

Huebsch, Bill. *The General Directory for Catechesis in Plain English*
Twenty Third Publications, Mystic, CT
An outstanding paraphrase of the Directory with a brief study guide
for group use.

Huebsch, Bill. *Whole Community Catechesis in Plain English*
Twenty Third Publications, Mystic, CT
Gives a complete overview of whole community catechesis and what
it means by offering concrete suggestions for a step-by-step process
for implementing this catechetical model.

Inkel, Maxine, S.L. *What Would Jesus Do? A Catechist's Guide to
Discipline*
Twenty Third Publications, Mystic, CT
These down-to-earth and upbeat reflections offer the example of
Jesus as the inspiration for an approach to discipline.

Wezeman, Phyllis. *100 Creative Teaching Techniques for Religion Teachers*
Twenty Third Publications, Mystic, CT
Provides catechists with a wealth of possibilities for telling and
reviewing the stories of faith and Scripture with their classes.

Of Related Interest

How to Be a Great DRE
Six Steps for Catechetical Leaders
Gail Thomas McKenna

This experienced DRE shares her ideas and encouragement with those who are striving to provide the best for their parish faith formation program. She offers concrete suggestions, sample forms, organizational tools and more.
1-58595-229-X, 96 pp, $14.95

30 Rituals and Prayer Services
for Catechist and Teachers Meetings
Alison J. Berger

These beautifully prepared rituals and services provide meaningful ways for catechists and teachers to celebrate their ministry. Themes include liturgical seasons, aspects of catechetical ministry, the beatitudes, and the sacraments. Each service is a complete prayer experience suitable for meetings as well as for days of prayer and reflection.   1-58595-267-2, 72 pp, $14.95

How Each Child Learns
Using Multiple Intelligence in Faith Formation
Bernadette Stankard

Here Bernadette Stankard shows catechists how the theory of multiple intelligence can be used to creatively teach religion. She introduces readers to this theory and then expands on how this approach can broaden a child's experience of God. Stankard provides inventive suggestions and practical approaches. This book is a great resource for parents, catechists, and teachers.
1-58595-269-9, 120 pp, $10.95

Teaching Self-Discipline to Children
15 Essential Skills
Barbara C. Vasiloff

Barbara Vasiloff identifies fifteen self-discipline skills and suggests concrete, classroom-tested ways to empower children to take responsibility for their behavior. In this hands-on book there are sample forms, worksheets, poems, songs, activities, as well as guided meditations to use with children.
1-58595-272-9, 96 pp, $14.95

TWENTY-THIRD PUBLICATIONS
185 WILLOW STREET • PO BOX 180 • MYSTIC, CT 06355
TEL: 1-800-321-0411 • FAX: 1-800-572-0788
Bayard E-MAIL: ttpubs@aol.com • www.twentythirdpublications.com